WHAT
ABOUT
THE DEVIL?

WHAT ABOUT THE DEVIL?

A Study of Satan in the Bible and Christian Tradition

FaithQuestions SERIES

Douglas E. Wingeier

ABINGDON PRESS
NASHVILLE

WHAT ABOUT THE DEVIL?
A Study of Satan in the Bible and Christian Tradition

Copyright © 2006 by Abingdon Press

This book is printed on acid-free, elemental chlorine-free paper.

ISBN: 0-687-33094-7

06 07 08 09 10 11 12 13 14 15—10 9 8 7 6 5 4 3 2 1

MANUFACTURED IN THE UNITED STATES OF AMERICA

CONTENTS

HOW TO USE
What About the Devil?
A Study of Satan in the Bible and Christian Tradition

What About the Devil? explores understandings of Satan as presented in the Bible and in Christian tradition and how these understandings inform Christian life. It invites participants to consider such questions as:

- What does the Bible say to us about Satan? How has Satan, or the devil, been understood in Christian history?
- What is the connection between Satan and evil? Between Satan and disease?
- What is exorcism? What are demons? Can we be possessed by Satan?
- What are contemporary understandings of Satan? How do such understandings inform our daily Christian life?
- How do I combat the forces of Satan?

This book is designed for use in any of three settings: 1) adult Sunday school; 2) weekday adult groups; and 3) retreat settings. It can also provide a meaningful resource for private study.

Sunday School: What About the Devil? may be used on Sunday mornings as a short-term, seven-week study. Sunday morning groups generally last 45 to 60 minutes. If your group would like to go into greater depth, you can divide the chapters and do the study for longer than seven weeks.

Weekday Study: If you use What About the Devil? in a weekday study, we recommend 90-minute sessions. Participants should prepare ahead by

˙reading the content of the chapter and choosing one activity for deeper reflection and study. A group leader may wish to assign these activities.

Retreat Study: You may wish to use WHAT ABOUT THE DEVIL? in a more intense study, like a weekend retreat. Distribute the books at least two weeks in advance. Locate and provide additional media resources and reference materials, such as Bible dictionaries and commentaries. If possible, provide a computer with an Internet connection in order to do online research. Tell participants to read WHAT ABOUT THE DEVIL? before the retreat begins. Start on Friday with an evening meal or refreshments followed by gathering time and worship. Discuss Chapter 1. Cover Chapters 2, 3, 4, and 5 on Saturday and Chapters 6 and 7 on Sunday. Develop a schedule that includes time for breaks, meals, and personal reflection of various topics in the chapters. End the retreat with closing worship on Sunday afternoon.

Leader/Learner Helps

Leader/learner helps are located in boxes near the relevant main text. They include a variety of discussion and reflection activities. Include both the gathering and closing worship activities in each session of your study, and choose from among the other leader/learner helps to fit the time frame you have chosen for your group.

The activities in the leader/learner helps meet the needs of a variety of personalities and ways of learning. They are designed to stimulate both solitary reflection and group discussion. An interactive and informal environment will foster a dynamic interchange of ideas and demonstrate the value of diverse perspectives. While the readings may be done in the group, reading outside of the session will enrich individual reflection and group discussion.

The Role of the Group Leader

The group leader facilitates gathering and closing worship, organizes the group for each session, monitors the use of time so that adequate attention is given to all major points of the chapter, and encourages an atmosphere of mutual respect and Christian caring. He or she should participate fully in the study as both learner and leader. The same person may lead all the sessions, or each session may have a different leader.

INTRODUCTION

"Do you renounce the spiritual forces of wickedness, reject the evil powers of this world, and repent of your sin?" In this question, which is included in the baptismal rituals of many Christian denominations, we find the dilemma with which Scripture writers, church fathers, and theologians of all stripes have struggled down through the ages. In fact, it was an issue for the mythmakers of ancient Sumerian, Babylonian, Egyptian, Greek, and Roman times as well. And it's a problem for us, too.

The issue is, Where do sin and evil come from? Do the "spiritual forces of wickedness" and the "evil powers of this world" bring misfortune upon us and lead us astray? Or do our own willfulness, the bad choices we make, our selfishness, and our greed compose the essence of sin? If bad things are caused by some supernatural power called Satan or the devil, then where does such a being get its power? If God is all good and all-powerful, then why is evil allowed? Does God permit it? Or are God's power and goodness somehow limited by an independent evil force that contends with God to control the human soul and shape history?

On the other hand, if evil is our own doing and we are free to avoid it, then why do we so often sin by making wrong choices? Is it simply a matter of misusing our free will, or are we irresistibly swayed by something sinister lurking within our hearts? Did "the devil make us do it"? Is this just a cop-out from taking responsibility for our actions? Or are we struggling against a supernatural, satanic power much greater than our own?

The baptismal vow allows for both possibilities, and it calls on us to renounce the one and repent of the other. In the next vow, we read the following pledge: "Do you accept the freedom and power God gives you to resist evil, injustice, and oppression in whatever forms they present themselves?" This implies that we, by God's grace, do have within ourselves the power to contend against evil, whether it appears in human or super-human form.

In the third vow, we read, "Do you confess Jesus Christ as your Savior, put your whole trust in his grace, and promise to serve him as your Lord, in union with the Church which Christ has opened to people of all ages, nations, and races?" Here we are offered the resource and support for dealing with sin and evil—a Savior who forgives, a Lord to serve, and a global, inclusive community of faith to sustain us in the struggle.

These three vows suggest a progression of thought that will guide this study on Satan. In each of our seven sessions, we will look at one or more aspects of the power of evil, discuss how it affects our lives and how we deal with it, and explore the resources of faith that provide support and guidance in the encounter. Our focus will be to understand the place of Satan in Scripture and Christian tradition and to provide faith resources for the struggle against evil in our souls and our society. We will explore a number of issues of good and evil, examine various understandings of Satan, and identify ways our beliefs about Satan can affect our daily practice of Christian faith.

Jesus used the words "Get behind me, Satan!" to rebuke Peter for trying to deter him from going to Jerusalem to confront the principalities and powers (see Matthew 16:23). The aim of this book is to provide resources for us so that we, like Jesus, can put temptations and fears behind us in our journey toward faithful discipleship, in the struggle against evil, and in our efforts to fulfill God's purpose for our lives.

In Chapter 1, **The Problem of Evil,** we look at some major Old and New Testament references to the devil as well as some interpretations offered in church history. Several roles and titles assigned to Satan are described. Questions of the connection between Satan and evil, disease, and human sin are discussed, along with whether Satan is a personalized embodiment of evil or merely an abstract force. The good news that God overcomes Satan and evil through Christ's death and resurrection is emphasized.

Satan as Tempter is the focus of Chapter 2, which explores the experience of temptation and appropriates faith resources for dealing with it. The serpent in the garden of Eden and Satan's temptation of Jesus in the wilderness provide a biblical background for exploring our own struggles with the devil's lures and ways of overcoming them. The resources of Scripture, prayer, and Christian community are offered as guidance and support for contending with temptation.

The relationship between God and Satan in biblical accounts, Christian literature, and human experience is the focus of Chapter 3, **Satan as Fallen Angel and Adversary.** The stories of Balaam in Numbers 22 and the king of Babylon in Isaiah 14, as well as Paul's reference to Satan disguised as an angel of light in 2 Corinthians 11, are the primary Scriptures explored. The nature of the battle between God and Satan is examined, and the theme of God as Sovereign over all, including principalities and powers (Ephesians 1), is emphasized.

Chapter 4, **Demon Possession and Exorcism,** relates the experience of the indwelling and expulsion of demons in biblical times and traditional societies to contemporary forms of mental illness and healing. The Gospel stories of Jesus casting out demons are the primary biblical resource, and the historical attribution of demon possession is explored, along with contemporary forms of emotional disturbance and spiritual malaise. The healing presence of Jesus offers the good news of salvation and wholeness to troubled persons in all times and places.

In Chapter 5, **The Antichrist and the End Times,** the background of the satanic figure of the antichrist in early church apocalypticism is explained, and contemporary dispensationalist teaching about the end times, as represented in the Left Behind Series, is analyzed. Jesus' teaching about the end is compared with that of other early writers. The positive theme of Christian hope for this and every age is highlighted.

Chapter 6, **The Devil in "the Other"—And in Us,** addresses our tendency to project evil onto "the other"—whether an enemy, a larger-than-life historical figure, or a supernatural force—and the corresponding reluctance to acknowledge our own sinful attitudes. We explore some of the guises in which Satan has appeared in Scripture, literature, and in our own experiences. Also discussed are questions of whether Satan is a force coming from within or outside us, as well as whether sin and evil are the doing of Satan or our own responsibility. A primary biblical reference is Paul's struggle with the power of sin and the victory of freedom through "the Spirit of life in Christ Jesus" (Romans 7:14–8:2).

The final chapter, **Contending Against Satan,** offers strength for the ongoing struggle against evil. Among the biblical passages explored are Jesus' statement to Peter, "Get behind me, Satan!" (Matthew 16:23); Jesus' provision of power over Satan (Luke 9 and 10); the urging of James to resist the devil and of First Peter to be watchful and steadfast; and, above all, the description of "the whole armor of God" for protection against the power of Satan (Ephesians 6:10-20).

An effort is made throughout to focus on straightforward answers to the troublesome questions that challenge our faith. Why do bad things happen? Why do we sin? Does the devil really exist? How do we defeat him? How can the Bible and Christian faith help us in the struggle against evil? What offers hope for the future? By God's grace, may this study strengthen our resolve to "renounce the spiritual forces of wickedness, reject the evil powers of this world, and repent" of our sin with renewed vigor and commitment.

CHAPTER 1
THE PROBLEM OF EVIL

Where does evil come from?

Focus: This chapter examines the manifestations and sources of evil in our lives and world, as well as the roles assigned to Satan as the cause.

Disaster as Evil

Thad and Edna Jones bought their simple, one-story frame house fifty-five years ago. Through the years, they raised their family in it and saw no need to move. It was situated near a river that supplied the power for the plant that Thad worked in until his retirement five years ago. During heavy rains and spring thaws, the river sometimes got quite high, but it never overflowed its banks—not until this year.

Three months ago, two successive hurricanes brought torrential rains and high winds. Flood waters raged through their small town, rose to a height of five feet inside their home, and destroyed everything. It all happened so fast that furniture, family heirlooms, photo albums, clothing—nothing could be saved. Their home was damaged beyond repair.

Thad and Edna were devastated. They had no flood insurance. Government funds were limited and would cover only a fraction of their loss. Their income from social security covered only their everyday expenses. They had no margin or savings to cope with such an overwhelming catastrophe, so they could not hope to rebuild or relocate. Their daughter had died in childhood, and they were alienated from their son, so no help would be forthcoming from that quarter. Now, in their declining years, when they had hoped to live out their lives in contentment, they had lost everything and had nowhere to turn. Why did such an evil calamity descend on them at this time in their lives?

Thad and Edna's suffering could have many root causes. Perhaps they bought too close to the river. Maybe they should have made better financial plans, like purchasing flood insurance or saving money for a "rainy day." Perhaps Thad's company was at fault for building workmen's housing in a flood plain and/or not paying enough in wages and pensions so they could handle such a disaster. Maybe the government did not provide sufficient relief. Wasteful human consumption, negligence, greed, and lack of concern for environmental issues such as dependence on fossil fuels and cutting of old-growth forests may have contributed to the global warming that is causing increasingly violent, unpredictable weather patterns.

> What or who do you think is responsible for the disaster and suffering that have afflicted Thad and Edna?

Some would call the hurricanes "acts of God." Others would attribute the disaster to Satan as the source of all evil in the world.

Job: Satan as Adversary

The calamity that has befallen Thad and Edna and the question it raises—why do the innocent suffer?—are precisely those confronted in the Book of Job. Job is the work of several authors, compiled in the fifth or fourth century B.C. The prose prologue (Chapters 1 and 2) and epilogue (42:7-17) probably were written before the poetic discourses (3:1–42:6),

14

which may be an Israelite revision of an older Canaanite or Edomite epic poem expressing their views on the age-old problem of evil.[1]

The prologue tells an intriguing story about faith, suffering, and the human response to the inexplicable. It describes Job as a man, both pious and prosperous, who has many children, lands, livestock, and servants. Wealthy, respected, and faithful, he is well-known in his region. The remainder of Chapter 1 describes how God and Satan (here seen as an "adversary" or "accuser" rather than "the evil one") consider the character of Job. Satan taunts God by saying that Job is faithful only because he is richly blessed. God thinks otherwise and gives Satan the power to take away all Job has. Job tears his clothing in anguish yet persists in praising God. Not satisfied, Satan wants "skin for skin" (2:4). God, still believing in Job's uprightness, allows Satan to afflict Job's body under the condition of sparing his life. Thus, Satan is depicted as the member of God's heavenly court who—with God's permission—is responsible for inflicting evil and suffering upon humanity.

At the time Job was written, material blessings were thought to be God's rewards for good behavior, while curses or hardships indicated sin. Into this belief system came Job, a man magnificently blessed yet tormented with the loss of all he had. There he is, an upright, blameless man, exhibiting the classical Eastern signs of grief (1:20-21a; 2:8). Yet he continues to praise God. How can this be? For Job, all things come from God (1:21b), even

> Read Job 1 and 2. What, if anything, challenges you in these Scriptures? How do you respond to the notion that blessings are God's rewards for good behavior and curses are Satan's punishment for bad behavior? Have you been treated unfairly by life or felt that you deserved your good fortune? What is the source of evil and suffering—God, Satan, or human action? How does your faith help you reconcile good things happening to bad people and bad things happening to good people?

though the writer attributes his misfortune to Satan. Understanding that the gifts of love and devotion bring the risk of heartache and violence, Job affirms that God is always present, even in the direst of circumstances.

But his wife feels differently. Enraged, she compels Job to "get in touch with his anger" and lash out at God, urging her husband to take charge and do something. But calling her foolish, Job dismisses his one remaining family member while preserving his integrity. Aching, grieving, and scraping at his sores, Job remains faithful to God, who "gave, and . . . has taken away (1:21).

In Chapter 23, Job is still struggling with loss and grief and the question of why misfortune has befallen him, a righteous man. His friends (see Chapters 4–5, 8, 11) have urged him to examine his life and repent, for misfortune is a sure sign of sin. But he has rejected their counsel. He is confident that this traditional Hebrew wisdom does not apply to him because he is innocent. Job answers Eliphaz's admonishment to repent with the words "Today also my complaint is bitter" (23:2). But he steadfastly refuses to repent of sins he has not committed. He will not betray his integrity nor succumb to pressure. His heart is pure.

> Read Job 23:1-9, 16-17. When have you felt that God was absent from your life? When have you asked, sought, and knocked but got no response? How did you feel? What was blocking communication? How do you explain the presence of injustice in a world created by a righteous God?

Despite his great loss and oozing sores, Job believes that if God will grant him a trial, he can prove his innocence. Vindication will come if only God will listen. Job believes that God is a God of justice and compassion. If he can only explain his situation, surely God will pronounce him innocent and restore his well-being (23:3-7).

In the imagined trial, Job faces a problem: Where is God? Job looks left and right, forward and backward, but God is nowhere to be found (23:8-9). To Job, God's obscurity is as unimaginable as the loss of all he possessed. He has taken God's presence for granted. As trustworthy as the rise of the morning sun, God is immanent in Job's life. It is only in God's apparent absence that Job realizes he has presumed that God would always be there.

Job is struggling to hold on to his belief in a God of justice while facing incomprehensible injustice. How can a loving God allow suffering? How can God be on the side of the righteous when they are plagued by terrible, undeserved suffering? This conundrum—why the innocent suffer—spans the ages. In the story of Job,

> Read again Job 23:16-17. Have you ever felt similar fear and terror about God? What were the circumstances?

we see the timeless dilemma of how a just God can permit an unjust world. The author of the prologue blames it on Satan and God's permissive will. Job's friends say it is all his fault. But Job is not satisfied. Without a ready answer, he retreats into dread and trepidation (23:16-17). "God has made my heart faint; / the Almighty has terrified me," he moans.

Beginning in Chapter 38, the trial before God begins. Satan, sure that Job will rail at God, is waiting in the wings in breathless anticipation. Even if Job remains faithful to God, the question remains as to why he, an innocent man, has had to suffer. How can he restrain himself from cursing God now that he finally has his hearing?

Out of the whirlwind, God speaks to Job—but not with compassion and solace. In 13:23, Job had asked, "How many are my iniquities and my sins? / Make me know my transgression and my sin." But instead of giving a direct answer, God showers Job with a series of questions: "Who is this...?" "Where were you...?" "Who determined...?" "Do you know...?" "Can you...?" (38:2, 4, 5, 33, 34). God is challenging Job's impudence in asserting his innocence before the Almighty.

Job, God contends, is betraying his arrogance by challenging God's justice. As a mere human, Job's capacity for understanding the mysteries of the universe is exceedingly limited, while God's wisdom, power, and greatness are boundless. God had "laid the foundation," "loose[d] the cords of Orion," sent "forth lightnings," "put wisdom in the inward parts," and "number[ed] the clouds" (38:4, 31, 35-37). God is the almighty Creator. Whatever comes into being does so solely at God's command.

Job 38:31-41 records feats that Job, a mere human, could never accomplish. Can he provide rain and lightning? Scatter the stars in the heavens? Give understanding to the mind? Hunt for the lion?

> Read Job 38:1-11, 31-41. Do you believe that both order and chaos are part of God's plan? Do evil, injustice, and suffering really serve a good end? How does the illusion that we are in control of the universe and our destiny undermine our trust in God? What signs of this human arrogance do you see in our society? How can we tell the difference between the work of Satan and the purpose of God? How would our lives be different if we acknowledged God's sovereignty and surrendered our lives to God's will?

Provide the raven with its prey? Job is impotent, but God is able. Job is being brought down to size, humbled before the awesome majesty of the Creator. God is reminding Job that after all, it is God—not he—who is in charge. God is the Creator, and Job the creature. To question such truths only shrouds the grandeur and mystery of God and the universe. What seems like evil and injustice to finite Job is in reality a part of God's master plan.

Not only do God's questions remind Job of the order of creation and his place in it, but they also recall that amid order, there is also chaos. God inquires, "Who shut in the sea with doors / when it burst out from the womb?" (38:8). Put in the mouth of the Almighty, yet another explanation of evil is offered here. Even though at the time we, like Job and the Joneses, cannot see or accept it, chaos, evil, and injustice are really expressions of God's good purpose. As Paul put it, "We know that all things work together for good for those who love God, who are called according to his purpose" (Romans 8:28).

The tension in the story thus far has been whether good will triumph over evil. Who will win the contest for Job's soul—God or Satan? Will Job break under the weight of his misfortunes and curse God, or will his faith continue to sustain him? The climax comes in Chapter 42. Job's answer to God begins with a confession of God's omnipotent power: "I know that you can do all things" (42:2). In response to God's speech from the whirlwind, Job acknowledges his limitations by conceding that he has been talking nonsense. From confession he moves to a declaration that he "had heard of you by the hearing of the ear, / but now my eye sees you; / therefore I despise myself" (42:5-6). To be in the presence of God's absolute goodness requires a humble recognition of one's own sinfulness and finitude. Job then ends his soliloquy in penitence for arrogantly demanding God's response.

Thus, in the end, Job lives up to his reputation as "blameless and upright, one who feared God and turned away from evil" (1:1). The epilogue describes how his faithfulness is finally rewarded with the restoration of his fortunes and family. Still, there remains the lingering question: Why was this innocent, upright man subjected to so much suffering? Does God hand out suffering just to prove God's strength in a contest?

Questions and answers about evil and suffering are never simple. The wisdom does not come from living a neat story with a happy ending. The drama of Job was written to refute the theology of Deuteronomy that was widely accepted in the post-exilic period: The righteous are rewarded with material blessings, and the wicked are punished with pain and trouble. As expounded by Job's friends, this theory was simply not

18

adequate to explain what happened to Job and to the people of Israel and Judah, whose lands were seized, families separated, holy places desecrated, and who themselves were dragged off into exile. Instead, wisdom and faith come from meeting God in the encounter with affliction and ambiguity. It is not that there are no answers to human misfortune; it is that we grow and learn best from experiencing God in the midst of the fray.

In the story of Job, we see four responses to the problem of evil and suffering:

> Which of the four responses to the problem of evil and suffering best addresses the need of Thad and Edna Jones? Do these ideas help us deal with the problem of evil and suffering, or do they still leave us with nagging questions? How do we live with this ambiguity?

• Suffering is inflicted by Satan, with God's permission, as a test of faith.
• Suffering is the inevitable result of sin and disobedience.
• Suffering is allowed by God in order to confront human arrogance, to induce humility and trust, and to evoke wisdom.
• Suffering is a part of God's plan, with a hidden good purpose for us to discern.

Elsewhere in Scripture

Job is not the only place in Scripture where the problem of evil emerges. In Genesis 6–9, a catastrophic flood destroys all of creation. Only one righteous man, his family, and animal pairs are spared. This is God's doing—punishment because "the wickedness of humankind was great in the earth" (6:5). The disobedience was not just human, though, because "the sons of God [divine beings descended from God's heavenly court—forerunners of the 'fallen angel' that became Satan] went in to the daughters of humans" and produced Nephilim (the warlike giants of ancient Near Eastern mythology), thereby breaching the God-ordained boundary between heaven and earth (Genesis 6:4). Thus, both natural calamity and human violence are traced to a combination of human willfulness and superhuman interference.[2]

In Matthew 2:16-18, a horrendous massacre is perpetrated on innocent children by an enraged King Herod, portrayed as the personification of evil—the cunning, cruel adversary of John the Baptizer, Jesus, and all things good. Here, evil is brought about by a wicked person holding near-absolute political power—a type of the "principalities, ... powers, ... rulers of the darkness of this world, ... spiritual wickedness in high places" against which the people of faith must struggle (Ephesians 6:12, KJV). Satanic powers like this, while apparently only human, take on a larger-than-life aura that inspires awe, fear, and dread but also stirs courageous resistance.

Hence, the power of evil—whether personified in Satan, an authoritarian ruler, or mythical superhuman beings—is seen in Scripture as a force vying with God for the bodies and souls of human beings. It preys upon the faithful (Job 1:12; 1 Peter 5:8), seeking to lead them astray. In defiance of God, it claims authority and dominion over humans and all the world (Luke 4:6; Acts 26:18; John 12:31, 14:30, 16:11). It is variously identified as "the god of this world" (2 Corinthians 4:4), "the accuser" (in Hebrew, *ha-satan*, the Satan), a murderer, and "the lawless one." Its tactics include deceiving, seducing, tricking, slandering, lying, and outwitting (Job 1:9-11; John 8:44; 2 Corinthians 2:11; 2 Thessalonians 2:9). It also is accused of inflicting disease (Job 2:7), resisting God and accusing humans (Zechariah 3:1-2), undermining good influence and sowing weeds (i.e., infiltrating bad people) among the faithful (Matthew 13:38-39), and instigating the treachery of Judas (John 13:2).

> Look up the Scripture references mentioned in this paragraph. In the case of each, ask:
>
> - What is the trait or tactic identified? What makes it evil?
> - Is this the work of human beings or a superhuman force?
> - How do we see this manifested in our lives and society? How does it affect us?
> - How do we resist it? Cite specific instances.

Names of Satan

Scripture assigns various titles to the satanic figure or evil influence that affects and seeks to control our lives. In the Eden story, it is a serpent that tempts Adam and Eve to partake of the forbidden fruit (Genesis 3:1-15). This image suggests a being of guile and deceit who entices us into arrogance, disobedience, and misleading assumptions. Matthew 4:1-3 refers to the devil as a tempter. In Matthew 12:24, we find the name

Beelzebul, the "ruler of the demons." This name is a reference to Baal-zebub, a god worshiped by the Philistines at Ekron (2 Kings 1:2-16). The name originally meant "lord of the lofty abode" but later was altered to "lord of flies" and, finally, to "lord of dung."[3] In Matthew 12:43-45, it names a homeless, wandering, unclean spirit that seeks to inhabit and corrupt our hearts. Matthew 13:19 refers to "the evil one," who stealthily steals the fragile seeds of faith sown in the human heart.

Paul speaks of the "god of this world," who blinds unbelievers to the truth of the gospel and the glory of God (2 Corinthians 4:3-4), and Beliar (2 Corinthians 6:15), an evil spirit mentioned in other early literature, who is subordinate to Satan. Peter identifies "your adversary the devil," who prowls around like a lion looking for unwitting souls to snatch away and devour (1 Peter 5:8). And John of Patmos speaks with vivid imagery of the "angel of the bottomless pit" (in Hebrew, *Abaddon*; in Greek, *Apollyon*—Revelation 9:11; see Job 26:6; Proverbs 15:11), a name that means "destruction" and refers to the depths of Sheol, the place of the dead. John also refers to the "accuser of our comrades" (Revelation 12:10). Some of these names come out of ancient Greek, Roman, and Near Eastern mythology, while others simply describe the way the early Christians experienced the corrupting, divisive, hostile forces around them.[4]

The figure of Satan has continued to play a prominent role in Christian theology and literature down through history. Neil Forsyth in *The Old Enemy* and Elaine Pagels in *The Origin of Satan* provide detailed historical accounts of the development of the idea of Satan and his angels in Canaanite, Babylonian, Persian, Egyptian, Greek, and Roman mythology, as well as in Jewish, Essene, Gnostic, and early Christian doctrine. Early church fathers Irenaeus, Justin Martyr, Tertullian, Origen, and Augustine each in his own way employed and refined the figure of Satan in their battles with the Gnostic, Marcionite, Manichaean, and Pelagian heresies.

Satan in Literature

In later centuries, Martin Luther, in a fit of temper, threw an inkwell at what he felt to be a figure of Satan hovering over his shoulder. The church leaders who conducted the Inquisition and the Salem witch trials accused persons of being possessed by and performing the nefarious works of the devil. Satan presides over Dante's *Inferno* at the center of hell. In John Bunyan's *Pilgrim's Progress,* Christian encounters the hideous monster

Apollyon in the Valley of Humiliation. In John Milton's *Paradise Lost,* a despairing and vengeful Satan causes the disobedience of Adam and Eve in the garden of Eden. Goethe's *Faust* strikes a fateful bargain with the devil. Stephen Vincent Benet's *The Devil and Daniel Webster* develops a similar theme. In *The Screwtape Letters,* C. S. Lewis mocks Satan with a variety of tongue-in-cheek admonitions to his nephew Wormwood on how to tempt and seduce the believer.

> Examine some of these references to Satan in religious and literary classics. Why does the figure of Satan keep recurring in such expressions of the human psyche? Do we view Satan as a real person, as do many of these thinkers? If so, how do we visualize and experience him? If not, how do we understand the reality he represents?

The final number in Walt Disney's film *Fantasia,* combining Modest Mussorgsky's "Night on Bald Mountain" with Franz Schubert's "Ave Maria," contrasts dark, sinister scenes of the devil and his demons with the tranquility and light of the sacred.

Satan Conquered by the Resurrection

In 1 Corinthians 15, Paul pronounces that in the resurrection of Christ, God "has destroyed every ruler and every authority and power. For he must reign until he has put all his enemies under his feet.... Thanks be to God, who gives us the victory through our Lord Jesus Christ" (15:24b-25, 57). The evil powers of Satan, sin, and death are brought under subjection to God's liberating power, a power that finds expression through the body of Christ. People who offer shelter, clothing, furniture, financial support, and physical labor in the tragedies like that of Thad and Edna become hands and feet in the defeat of evil. Two realizations offer life and hope in the face of evil: Material things are of fleeting value when compared with the love and comfort of family and friends, and trust in the

> How does the promise of victory through the resurrection of Jesus speak to the flood-stricken plight of Thad and Edna? To us? What practical help and hope does it offer?

companionship of God and God's people is more durable than physical security. In the struggle against darkness and evil in which Job, the Joneses, and countless others throughout history have been engaged, the hope of victory lies with the promise of light and life offered by the risen Christ.

Closing Worship

Sing the hymn "I Know Whom I Have Believed." Offer sentence prayers of thanks for victories over Satan won in times gone by, for discernment of the subtle influence of the demonic in our lives, and for strength in the ongoing struggle against sin and evil.

Notes

[1] For more information, see *The Interpreter's Bible,* Vol. 3 (Abingdon Press, 1954); pages 878–79.

[2] See *Nephilim* in *The Interpreter's Dictionary of the Bible,* Vol. K–Q (Abingdon Press, 1962); page 536.

[3] From *Harper's Bible Dictionary,* edited by Paul J. Achtemeier (HarperSanFrancisco, 1985); page 86.

[4] Look up Revelation 9:11 at http://bible.crosswalk.com or http://www.studylight.org, under NAS with Strong's Numbers, for more information about the meaning of the words *Abaddon* and *Apollyon.*

CHAPTER 2
SATAN AS TEMPTER

What is the source of temptation,
and how do we handle it?

Focus: This chapter explores the experience of temptation and the faith
resources for dealing with it.

Gathering

Greet one another. Write down the first word or phrase that comes
to mind in response to each of these words:

1. need	9. compulsion
2. lure	10. attraction
3. urge	11. action
4. feeling	12. love
5. desire	13. drive
6. motive	14. seduction
7. intention	15. response
8. choice	16. want

Which of these come from within, and which from without? Which do
we associate with temptation? Which influence us the most? The least?

Pray together the following prayer: "God of strength and hope, be
with us as we study about temptation and the traditional role of Satan
as tempter. We pray as Jesus taught us to pray: (end this prayer with
the Lord's Prayer)."

Temptation at the Office

Ralph Everett is an accountant in a large corporation. Diligent, competent, and conscientious, he has been rewarded with a series of promotions, and now he is the assistant comptroller. In this position, he sees most of the company's operations and has access to all financial transactions. Recently, he has noticed that some of the numbers do not match, so he goes to his supervisor about it. "Make them match," he is told, "and don't mention this to anyone else." Ralph is troubled but does what he is told and keeps quiet. Gradually, the variances between what he knows to be accurate and the figures being fed to him become larger and more frequent. Again he goes to the senior comptroller, stressing that if these discrepancies come to light, all who are aware of them will be in big trouble. This time the response is more pointed: "Cover this up and you'll be handsomely rewarded; expose it and you'll lose your job."

Now Ralph is sure that something unethical—if not illegal—is going on. He shares his concern with his wife, Nancy, who becomes frightened. "What can you do, Ralph?" she asks. "I'm in a bind," he replies. "If I spill the beans, who knows who may be involved or how they'll react? I'd be fired and out on the street—with credit card bills, college tuition, and mortgage payments piling up. The company could be investigated and become subject to lawsuits. Our stock value could plummet, and investors could lose a lot of money. On the other hand, if I keep mum, someone else could spot this. When it all blows up, I'll be implicated along with those above me, and I'll have a lot of explaining to do." "Yes," sighs Nancy, "if they bribe you to continue covering this up, we could pay off our debts, get our kids through college, and salt away enough to retire early and build our dream house. But if you blow the whistle…what will we do?" "I just don't know," moans Ralph.

> What temptation is confronting Ralph? What are his options? What are the consequences of each? Out of the sixteen words to which you responded at the beginning of class, which are relevant to Ralph's situation? Write up the ones mentioned, together with your written responses to each. Is Ralph's temptation coming to him from without or within? What might Satan be saying to him? What might the voice of God be urging? What temptations of this or other types do we face?

The Bible contains two well-known temptation stories: Adam and Eve's encounter with the serpent in the garden of Eden (Genesis 3:1-7) and Jesus' battle with Satan in the wilderness (Luke 4:1-13; see also Mark 1:12-13; Matthew 4:1-11), plus a host of briefer references.

Temptation in the Garden

The story of the Fall occurs in the J, or Yahwist, account of Creation, so called because it uses the name *Yahweh* for God. It was authored between the tenth and eighth centuries B.C. and tells the epic story of divine Creation, human rebellion, God's judgment in the Flood, and God's action to redeem fallen humanity through the people of Abraham and Moses. The Eden temptation story begins with a serpent sowing seeds of doubt in human minds (Genesis 3:1-2), continues with a defiant challenge to God's intention (3:3-5), and culminates with the first couple succumbing to the irresistible enticements of willful liberty (3:6-7).

The serpent is identified as a "wild animal" that had been created by God and named by humans. It is described as "more crafty" (in Hebrew, *arum*) than other animals, which makes a linguistic connection with "naked" (in Hebrew, *arummim*),[1] the blissful state the couple were in before the Fall (2:25) but became embarrassed about soon after (3:7). Temptation thus involves "exposure" to seductive influences that entice us to disobey God's commandments, reach beyond our limits, and suffer disastrous consequences. The Old Testament offers no further identification of the serpent, but the apocryphal Wisdom of Solomon (2:23-24) likens it to the devil, as does the Book of Revelation (12:9; 20:2), the latter equating *serpent* with *dragon*.

The Genesis story focuses not on the serpent, though, but on the human response to its guile. By implication, the serpent represents external influences offering choices that draw us away from God's presence and purpose. The tree of the knowledge of good and evil is the lure to know all there is to know, whether good for us or not. The serpent is the agent for making the options attractive. Initially, the serpent is not a crafty rogue but just a casual observer of the human situation, helping the woman clarify what God had forbidden. After Eve explains the situation, the serpent brashly pooh-poohs her fears, thereby subtly encouraging her to take the risk. To embark on the quest for full knowledge would result not in death but in greater awareness, deeper wisdom, and enhanced status on a par with God. With the aid of the serpent, she realizes that the knowledge would be tasty, attractive, and enriching. So she and Adam take and eat, then become vulnerable and defensive and seek to hide. The rest is history, as the saying goes—theirs, ours, and the world's. Thus, the serpent as tempter—only much later identified with Satan—is the facilitator that encourages human discontent with the status quo, willful pride, defiance of arbitrary authority, and exploration of the dangerous unknown.

Paul offers guidelines for sexual morality in 1 Corinthians 7. In verse 5, he urges his readers to devote themselves to prayer "so that Satan may not tempt you because of your lack of self-control." Here, the tempter is one who takes advantage of the undisciplined, not just the curious, like Adam and Eve. And resistance to his insidious influence is strengthened by the power of corporate prayer. In 1 Thessalonians 3:5, Paul also refers to the tempter, whom he fears has caused his converts to depart from the faith, thereby undercutting his evangelistic efforts.

Do you think the Fall was due more to the wiles of the serpent or the choices that the humans made? Was the temptation what the tree offered, what the serpent promised, or what the humans desired? What in the heart of the first humans made them want to take the fruit of the forbidden tree? Which of the words in the association test apply to their situation? Why do you think God forbade them to seek this knowledge? In our experience of temptation, what compares to the tree? The serpent? The act of seeking and taking? The result? What would each of these be for Ralph and Nancy Everett?

Then, in 2 Corinthians 11:2-4, the apostle refers back to the Eden story, likening his opponents—either Judaizers imposing the Law on Gentile converts or Gnostics claiming special spiritual knowledge—to the cunning serpent who beguiled Eve. His use here of the words *marriage to one husband* and *chaste virgin* recalls the parallel drawn by the prophet Hosea between sexual and spiritual infidelity and intimates that the tempter Satan, the temptress Eve, and by extension all women are somehow responsible for the

In your early hearing of the Eden story, were you led to connect the serpent with Satan as tempter? Eve as temptress? Sin with seduction? The knowledge of good and evil with heresy? Unbelief/heresy with disobedience/sin? How do you view these matters now?

27

human predicament. This oft-repeated accusation has resulted in no end of misery for generations of women. Thus began the link between the serpent/Satan, the first woman/Eve, heresy, and sexual promiscuity, which led in later centuries to the oppression of women and the atrocities of the Inquisition, anti-Semitism, and the Salem witch trials. In the latter, those with the courage to disagree with orthodoxy and defy hierarchy were tortured on the rack and burned at the stake. In these gross aberrations of Christian faith, those seeking to oppose Satan perversely ended up serving his wicked ends.

Temptation in the Desert

Many in Jesus' time expected the Messiah to be a powerful political leader, restoring Israel to its former greatness. Some thought he would be a priestly figure, purifying the nation with high standards of ritual holiness. These external expectations combined with Jesus' inner temptation to use his power to meet his own needs. The desert temptation scene shows what Jesus rejects and what he accepts among several personal and political options for his vocation as the Son of God. Empowered by the Holy Spirit, he is also severely pressed by a presence identified as Satan, who shrewdly manipulates his needs for food, power, and security (Luke 4:1-2).

Jesus is hungry after a lengthy fast. If he wants, he can turn a stone into bread (Luke 4:3-4). Since God had provided manna in the wilderness (Exodus 16), why should Jesus not do the same for himself? He responds with Scripture: "One does not live by bread alone" (Luke 4:4; see Deuteronomy 8:3). He will need not just physical sustenance but spiritual strength as well for the mission that lies ahead of him.

Read Luke 4:1-13, the Deuteronomy references, and Psalm 91:11-12. How do our needs for sustenance, power, and security affect our decisions and actions? How are these needs swaying Ralph and Nancy Everett? Which other factors from our opening word association might have influenced Jesus? The Everetts? Us? How does Satan as the tempter exploit these needs to divert us from our calling?

Next, Jesus is offered authority over worldly kingdoms—political power to accomplish any end (Luke 4:5-7). But, knowing he cannot serve two masters, he rejects this temptation with a second Scripture calling him to worship and serve God alone (Luke 4:8; see Deuteronomy 6:13).

28

Power corrupts, and should he become enamored with realms and armies, he will be diverted from his primary calling: sharing the love of God. Foiled thus far, the devil mimics Jesus' use of Scripture, quoting Psalm 91:11-12, which promises that God will protect the faithful with special power (Luke 4:9-11). Jesus replies that he cannot test God this way (Luke 4:12), referring to yet another Scripture (Deuteronomy 6:16). The wiles of the devil have been repulsed for now, but Satan is not through with him and will dog him throughout the remainder of his brief ministry (Luke 4:13).

The Scriptures Jesus uses here come from a key section of Deuteronomy and thus lodge his ministry squarely within his Jewish heritage. His obedience, however, contrasts with the behavior of his ancestors, whose complaints and idolatry grieved God during their forty years in the wilderness. The temptation shows him to be a prophet like Moses (Exodus 34:28) and Elijah (1 Kings 19:8), who also fasted and prayed for forty days in the desert. Right after the temptation, Jesus cited Isaiah 61:1-2 in the synagogue at Nazareth to clarify what he had come to do: bring the good news of God's love to the poor. Satan had not deterred him from this goal, though those threatened by this mission would seek to do the devil's work by using all available means—including crucifixion—to defeat it.

Jesus' opening personal struggle with the devil prefigures his ongoing battle with the forces of evil throughout his ministry and foreshadows his final temptation on the cross. One criminal echoes the devil's words: "Are you not the Messiah? Save yourself and us!" (Luke 23:39). But Jesus does not invoke special powers or perform mighty works to save himself; instead, he is obedient to death in order to save others. His dying overcame evil and made it possible for all to have life in the

> **Discuss the following:**
>
> - How can Scripture be a resource for us in struggling with temptation?
> - What Scriptures might Ralph and Nancy consider in deciding how to resolve Ralph's ethical dilemma?
> - What Scriptures are called to mind by words in the association test like *need, feeling/feel, desire, choice/choose, compulsion/compel, action/act, love, drive/driven, seduction/seduce, want*? Look these words up in a concordance, find the Scriptures containing them, and discuss how these might be resources in our struggle with temptation.

resurrection. The same power that sustained Jesus in his lifelong battle with evil can also guide and empower us in our encounters with temptation.

Temptation in the Old Testament

Many other passages of Scripture touch on the connection between Satan, the serpent, and temptation and suggest ways of resisting this influence. In 1 Chronicles 21 (written around 550 B.C., about the same time as Job), Satan is used to explain division in Israel's ranks. Five centuries before, King David had initiated an unpopular census as a basis for taxation. Joab, David's general, warned him that this was an evil thing. But David overrode his objections, and the census was carried out. By blaming this on *ha-satan*, or "an adversary"—a supernatural member of the heavenly court who covertly convinced David to commit this sin against Israel—rather than on David himself, the chronicler avoided condemning the king directly while making it clear the policy was wrong. Even though David soon repented of his sin, an angry God wreaked punishment on him and Israel, annihilating 70,000 in a plague and nearly destroying the city of Jerusalem. Thus, Satan as an adversary is portrayed as one who opposes the well-being of God's people.

Similarly, the prophet Zechariah, writing a few years later (520 B.C.), depicts Satan not as an evil power but as God's messenger who accuses humans of sin (3:1 and following). In the dispute between the exiles returning from Babylon and the rural inhabitants who had remained in the land, Zechariah takes the side of the returning refugees. But he reports a vision in which Satan is the spokesman for the locals and is obstructing the will of God. Satan thus is seen as diverting God's people from their true purpose or calling.

In Psalm 74:13-14 and Isaiah 27:1, God is pictured as slashing or crushing the dragon, the "fleeing serpent," or Leviathan in the sea, and feeding his remains to the animals. Leviathan was a legendary sea monster associated with Satan in the literature of both mythology and religion. He was clearly subject to God's sovereignty and would be destroyed in the end.[2]

Temptation in the New Testament

Moving to the New Testament, in Luke 10:19-20, Jesus tells the seventy disciples returning from an evangelistic mission, "See, I have given you authority to tread on snakes and scorpions, and over all the power of the enemy; and nothing will hurt you." He then suggests that God has caused the evil spirits to submit to them. Snakes and scorpions—symbols of evil and temptation—are subdued by the power of Jesus transmitted to his followers.

When Jesus begins explaining to his disciples his need to go to Jerusalem to confront the authorities, Peter, fearing for his safety, tries to dissuade him. But Jesus sharply rebukes his thick-witted disciple: "Get behind me, Satan! You are a stumbling block to me; for you are setting your mind not on divine things but on human things" (Matthew 16:23). Jesus then explains that his followers must "deny themselves and take up their cross and follow me" (Matthew 16:24). The Hebrew word for Satan is translated in the Septuagint (third century B.C. Greek translation) as *ho diabolos* (meaning the "obstructor" or "stumbling block"), from which come our words *devil* and *diabolical*.[3] In Matthew 16:23, the word *satanas* has the same sense. Jesus is saying that Peter, out of concern for his safety, is tempting him to abort his mission by obstructing his determination to go to Jerusalem. The same devil-induced anxiety about safety would block his followers—both then and now—from taking the risks that true discipleship demands.

Then, in Luke 22:31-32, Jesus tells Simon Peter that despite Satan's efforts to disturb him and his fellow disciples, he has prayed for them to have the strength to withstand his seductive influence. However, later that same night, Peter yields to the temptation to deny his relationship with Jesus, so Satan gains a temporary victory (22:54-62). But the tempter loses out in the end, as Peter goes on to become a stalwart leader and martyr in the early church.

In his closing words of encouragement to the Romans, Paul promises that "the God of peace will shortly crush Satan under your feet" (Romans 16:20). Only Satan-as-serpent could be trodden on in this fashion. It is interesting that it is the "God of peace" who will do away with the

> Read Luke 10:19-20, Matthew 16:21-23, Luke 22:31-34, Romans 16:20, and 1 Corinthians 10:13. What is Satan's role here? What does this represent about the experience of temptation? How does this reflect our own experiences of temptation? What resource for dealing with temptation does the passage offer? What guidance does it provide for the Everetts? For us?

tempter—a puzzling paradox of reconciling and violent images. The power of love is more than a match for wicked, subversive influence.

An even stronger promise is given in 1 Corinthians 10:13: "No temptation has seized you except what is common to man. And God is faithful; he will not let you be tempted beyond what you can bear. But when you are tempted, he will also provide a way out so that you can stand up under it" (NIV). God is more powerful than the tempter, standing with us in the midst of temptation—enabling us to resist, overcome, escape, and endure.

Temptation in Christian Literature

Satan the tempter appears often in later Christian literature. In *Paradise Lost,* John Milton speaks of "the infernal serpent; he it was, whose guile, / Stirred up with envy and revenge, deceiv'd / the mother of mankind."[4] In another passage, he depicts Satan as traversing the earth in fervent search of prey to entice into sin and eternal punishment. For Milton, the devil was a powerful, devious being using all his wiles to entrap humans and send them to their doom.

In *The Screwtape Letters,* C. S. Lewis presents a more urbane, genteel image of the tempter. In his letters to his nephew Wormwood, Screwtape/Satan suggests all sorts of subtle devices for wooing believers away from faithful practices of spiritual disciplines and adherence to doctrinal orthodoxy. In one passage, Screwtape urges Wormwood to induce distractions to prayer in these words: "Whenever they are attending to the Enemy Himself [i.e., God] we are defeated, but there are ways of preventing them from doing so. The simplest is to turn their gaze away from Him towards themselves. Keep them watching their own minds and trying to produce *feelings* there by the action of their own wills."[5]

In John Bunyan's *The Pilgrim's Progress,* the devil sends a whole procession of personified temptations to obstruct Christian's progress toward the Celestial Country, with names like Worldly Wiseman, Hypocrisy, Mistrust, Discontent, Superstition, Envy, Giant Despair, Ignorance, Littlefaith, Ignorance, Fearing, Self-will, and Prejudice.[6] James Russell Lowell commented that "if the devil takes a less hateful shape to us than to our fathers, he is as busy with us as with them," suggesting that though Satan may be imaged differently, the seductive power of evil is pervasive in every time and place. William Shakespeare had a similar thought when he said, "The devil hath power to assume a pleasing shape."[7]

On resisting temptation, the sages offer a range of advice:

* "Better shun the bait than struggle in the snare" (John Dryden).
* "God is better served in resisting a temptation to evil than in many formal prayers" (William Penn).
* "Some temptations come to the industrious, but all temptations attack the idle" (Charles Spurgeon).
* "The realization of God's presence is the one sovereign remedy against temptation" (Fénelon).

> Paraphrase each of these literary citations. Then state the means of overcoming temptation that each one suggests. How will each of these be helpful to the Everetts? To us in dealing with our temptations?

* "Great possessions and great want of them are both strong temptations" (Goethe).
* "Every temptation is an opportunity of our getting nearer to God" (J. Q. Adams).
* "An honest heart is not to be trusted with itself in bad company" (Richardson).
* "The devil is very near at hand to those who, like monarchs, are accountable to none but God for their actions" (Gustavus Adolphus).[8]

Closing

Sing the hymn "Yield Not to Temptation." Returning to the word association test, discuss the role each of these elements plays in the Everetts' dilemma and in our own temptations. Summarize the forms of strength and guidance provided for this struggle by the Scriptures and advice explored in this chapter. Pray for each other, asking for direction and help in resolving the issues that have been shared. Close with the Lord's Prayer, substituting "help us to resist temptation" for the traditional words.

Notes

[1] From *The New Interpreter's Bible*, Vol. 1 (Abingdon Press, 1994); page 359.

[2] See notes for Isaiah 27:1 and Psalm 74:14 in the *New Oxford Annotated Bible* (Oxford University Press, 2001).

[3] See *Harper's Bible Dictionary*, edited by Paul J. Achtemeier (HarperSanFrancisco, 1985); page 220.

[4] From *Paradise Lost and Other Poems*, by John Milton, edited by Maurice Kelley (Walter J. Black, 1943); page 92.

[5] From *The Screwtape Letters*, by C.S. Lewis (The MacMillan Company, 1943); page 25.

[6] See *The Pilgrim's Progress*, by John Bunyan (The John C. Winston Company, 1933).

[7] From *Forty Thousand Quotations, Prose and Poetical*, compiled by Charles Noel Douglas (Halcyon House, 1917); page 496.

[8] From *Forty Thousand Quotations, Prose and Poetical*; pages 1757–58.

CHAPTER 3
SATAN AS FALLEN ANGEL
AND ADVERSARY

Is Satan independent of or subordinate to God?

Focus: This chapter explores the relationship between God and Satan (good and evil) in biblical accounts, Christian and ancient Near Eastern traditions, and human experience.

Gathering

Comb through recent newspapers and magazines, and clip headlines and photos depicting current events of an evil nature. Stick these up on the wall in a crazy-quilt fashion to create the impression of a world gone awry.

Recite together the Apostles' Creed. How can we affirm these beliefs in the face of all that is going on in our world?

In the struggle between God and Satan, who is winning? How do we know?

When it seems like Satan is in control, what keeps us strong in our faith? Pray for insight to understand the issues raised in this session and for strength to combat the power of Satan in our everyday lives.

The Death of God, the Reign of Satan

Scattered through the memoirs of Hank (not his real name), a World War II veteran, are many references to God. Some are swear words, some mere idle exclamations, some petitions for protection and survival, some prayers of guilt and forgiveness for the death and destruction he is inflicting on soldiers and civilians alike. The longer he is in combat, the less hope he holds out for survival, and the more he wonders whether God cares. Once, in desperation he cries out, "Oh God! It's terrible! Please stop this war!" Finally, one of his prayers begins, "Dear God (if there is a God...)." Then, after three-plus years of near-constant combat, he concludes, "Perhaps, after God made the world, he just died—or maybe he just went away." The hell he had experienced in warfare had caused him to lose faith in even the existence of God. Satan had taken over and was running a world of horror and violation of all he had believed to be right and true.[1]

In *Night*, Elie Wiesel describes a death camp scene when three are hung for suspected sabotage—two men and a young boy:

> The three victims mounted together onto the chairs.
> The three necks were placed at the same moment within the nooses.
> "Long live liberty!" cried the two adults.
> But the child was silent.
> "Where is God? Where is He?" someone behind me asked.
> At a sign from the head of the camp, the three chairs tipped over.
> Total silence throughout the camp. On the horizon, the sun was setting....
> Then the march past began. The two adults were no longer alive. Their tongues hung swollen, blue-tinged. But the third rope was still moving; being so light, the child was still alive....
> For more than half an hour he stayed there, struggling between life and death, dying in slow agony under our eyes. And we had to look him full in the face.... His tongue was still red, his eyes not yet glazed.
> Behind me, I heard the same man asking:
> "Where is God now?"
> And I heard a voice within me answer him:
> "Where is He? Here He is—He is hanging here on this gallows."[2]

It was not a redemptive crucifixion Wiesel was talking about. It was the death of God—and of his faith in God. No loving God could exist and permit the kind of horror that was passing before his eyes. God was dead. The world was in Satan's hands. There was no hope.

The West family have finished supper in their country home a half mile up the road from an interstate exit and are watching TV. Suddenly they hear loud voices and stomping feet on the porch outside. Their front door is forced open, and two half-drunk strangers burst into their living room. Brandishing guns, they demand money. When the parents hesitate, the family—Carl and Esther, Grandma Ruth, and Stephen and Doris, ages fourteen and nine—are lined up against the wall and shot in cold blood. Neighbors find them the next morning in a pool of blood. The community is torn up; the Wests were solid citizens and active church members. The funeral draws a huge crowd. The two invaders are caught by police a few days later. In a trial that evokes high feelings in their small town, one is convicted and sentenced to death, the other to life imprisonment without parole. Months later, the execution takes place. Some feel justice has been served; others believe the taking of a human life, even by the state, is never justified.

What awful power leads men to murder total strangers in the sanctity of their own home? Why did the West family's devotion to God and high moral principles not protect them from evil? Why do some gain satisfaction from acts of revenge, even when legitimized by the justice system? Where was God that dreadful night? What allows Satan to reign in the hearts of men and out-of-the-way places?

Through the centuries, experiencing the overwhelming power of evil such as that encountered by the GI, the Jewish Holocaust victim, and the peaceful family has led people to agonize over the relationship between God and Satan. Is God dead? Asleep? Just absent for a while? After creating the world, did God abdicate responsibility and turn over the reins to the devil? Is Satan a rebellious fallen angel sent to earth to do God's bidding but gone astray to cause mischief? Is the evil that Satan causes actually a part of God's permissive plan? Are God and Satan two powers of equal strength vying for control of human lives and history, with the outcome still uncertain?

God and Satan: Some Theories

Philosophers and theologians have come up with a range of answers to these questions:

(1) Some say that neither God nor Satan is involved in the human situation. Humans are free to make their own choices, and the moral evils represented by wars, holocausts, and murders are nothing but our own doing. If we decided to, we could put an end to the kind of horror experienced by Hank, Elie Wiesel, and the West family. It's all up to us.

(2) Others explain that natural evils—floods, tornadoes, blights, earthquakes—are forms of punishment for the sins we commit. We clear-cut

forests, tamper with natural growth cycles, destroy species, and pollute streams; and natural disasters are the result. We bring these evils on ourselves, although it may be that God wills them as judgment or Satan instigates them by planting greed, envy, and spite in human hearts.

(3) Another approach is to say that God and Satan conspire together to allow or inflict these evils in order to discipline us. We become better persons through confronting and overcoming misfortune and disaster. Suffering produces character. Thus, Satan—willingly or unwillingly—serves God's good purpose.

(4) Still another explanation is that evil complements or serves as a necessary contrast to good. A painting is incomplete without the shadows and darker hues. The beauty and fullness of life is made up of both good and what appears to be bad. We recognize the good better when we can compare it with evil. We need the darkness in order to recognize the light. When we see the whole picture, we will understand. What felt to the soldier and the Holocaust survivor like the death of God was actually needed in order to glorify God through God's ultimate victory over evil. Thus, Satan fulfills a necessary function in God's overall plan.

(5) Others contend that Satan is an actual supernatural being or a larger-than-life force who has been turned loose to wreak havoc on the world. Some believe that this is with God's permission to serve a greater good. Others say that Satan is a power whom God is still struggling to defeat. Still others say that God's victory over Satan was won in Christ's death and

> Divide into five groups. Each should consider the encounters of the soldier, the Holocaust survivor, and the West family (or possibly a recent encounter with evil shared by someone in the group) in light of one of these approaches to the God-Satan relationship. After each group has explored its theory, choose one from each group to form a panel to discuss the situations of the soldier, the Holocaust survivor, the murdered family, and members' own encounters from the five perspectives. Consider these questions:
>
> • What light does each explanation throw on the situation? How satisfying is each?
> • How would the soldier and the survivor respond to each? What would we say to them? What one-sentence prayer would you have them say?

resurrection, but the "mopping up" operations are still going on—an affirmation of faith in defiance of the evidence "on the ground," so to speak.

The History of Satan in Ancient Mythology

Another perspective on the relationship between God and Satan can be gained from examining the idea of a supreme spirit of evil or enemy of God as it has appeared in the myths and beliefs of various cultures and religious expressions. In traditional or animistic religions, all happenings are attributed to either good or evil spirits who inhabit aspects of the plant and animal world, bless and afflict human beings, and are influenced by charms and incantations. Personifications of evil appear in the lady Nina and the dragon Tiamat in Babylonian lore, the serpent Apep among the Egyptians, the Titans and Prometheus in Greek mythology, Hel and Loki among the Teutons, and Ahi and Shiva in Hindu tradition. The struggle between good and evil finds its fullest expression in the dualism of Persian Zoroastrianism, in which the gods Ormazd and Ahriman, sources of good and evil, respectively, vie with one another for control of the universe.[3]

The History of Satan in the Bible

In the Judeo-Christian tradition, Satan as an evil being appears in the post-exilic period, showing the influence of the Persians on Jewish thinking. Traces of this idea go back much further, however. In Genesis 6:1-4, "the sons of God went in to the daughters of humans, who bore children to them. These were the heroes that were of old, warriors of renown." This is a reference to an old Near Eastern legend (also found in other ancient cultures) in which angels (inhabitants of the heavenly realm) cohabited with human beings and produced giant offspring who performed mighty deeds—both good and evil—upon the earth.

Then, in Judges 9:23, "God sent an evil spirit between Abimelech and the lords of Shechem" that caused treacherous dealings between them. In 1 Samuel 16:14, as we have seen, Saul is described as being tormented by "an evil spirit from the LORD." Later, Micaiah the prophet saw in a vision that "a spirit came forward and stood before the LORD" and offered to "be a lying spirit in the mouth of" Ahab's advisors, in order to entice him into a battle that would result in his defeat (1 Kings 22:19-23). In these instances, the demons are seen to be doing God's bidding, even though their acts are evil in nature. Hence, the satanic figures are clearly subordinate to God.

In the story of Balaam (Numbers 22:2–24:25), an angel of the Lord referred to as "satan"—which is not a proper name here and should be translated as "adversary"—not only carries out God's command but also offers an obstruction of a positive nature. The context is the Israelites' march toward conquest and occupation of Canaan. Moab's king Balak wants to stop their progress and summons the famed wizard Balaam to put a curse on Israel. Balaam accepts the assignment but has not reckoned with the power of Yahweh, Israel's God, whom the writer sees as supporting Israel's invasion. Balaam sets out to fulfill his commission but soon discovers that he is going where Yahweh does not want him to go. In his anger, Yahweh sends a messenger to obstruct Balaam's mission.

> Look up Judges 9:23, 1 Samuel 16:14, 1 Kings 22:19-23, and Numbers 22:22-35. With regard to each, discuss:
>
> • What is the context? How is Satan presented? How is God active?
> • What are the parallels to this in our life experience?
> • How do the Scriptures inform you about the relationship between God and Satan?

So "the angel of the LORD took his stand in the road as his adversary" (the Hebrew word that is translated "adversary" is *satan*). Balaam doesn't see the invisible adversary, but his donkey does and refuses to budge despite Balaam's beatings. When the adversary discloses himself to Balaam and rebukes him, Balaam sees the error of his ways and agrees to do God's will as explained by the adversary (22:22-35). Thus, in the Numbers tradition, the adversary was a messenger of God, a member of the heavenly court sent to block a wayward seer and set him back on the right track. Satan as adversary sometimes has a constructive effect.

Prior to the Exile, then, evil—whether misfortune or sin—was seen to be caused by God. (For example, see 1 Samuel 18:10, 2 Samuel 24:1, and Isaiah 6:10; 63:17.) But after the Jews' return from Babylon, God became more transcendent. Mediating angels appeared as agents of Satan, God's enemy, thereby separating evil from God. This we have seen in Zechariah 3:1-2, where Satan is presented as an adversary of Joshua, the high priest, and in Job 2:1, where Satan appears among the heavenly court but takes on a sinister mission. In the apocryphal literature of later Judaism, strongly influenced by Persian dualism, Satan has angelic servants who cause the serpent to seduce Eve, assist Satan to join with Eve to produce Cain, accuse humans before God, and introduce death into the human experience. (See Tobit 3:8; 6:14; Ecclesiasticus 21:27; Wisdom of Solomon 2:24; Psalms of Solomon 17:49; the Book of Enoch; and the Jewish Targums.) We have already described how Satan appears in the New Testament as *diabolos* (slanderer or accuser), tempter, evil one, enemy, Beelzebul, prince of demons, ruler over an evil world, and dragon or serpent.

The History of Satan in Church Tradition

In the early church, the influence of Greek and Roman polytheism is seen in the power of a realm of demons from which Christ is the Redeemer. Christ's death and resurrection made possible individual deliverance from Satan's bondage, but only in his second coming would Satan's final defeat be accomplished. In the debates between the orthodoxy of the early church fathers and the alternative interpretations of Gnosticism, Marcionism, dualistic Manichaeism, freewill Pelagianism, false doctrine, and sinful practice were traced to Satan, and the so-called "heretics" were labeled and persecuted as "children of the devil." Justin Martyr attributed misfortune to the agency of Satan rather than to God's will. Irenaeus proposed that the death of Christ was a ransom paid to the devil. Origen defended God's right to deceive the devil and suggested the eventual redemption of Satan, an idea later rejected. Persian dualism influenced Christian thought through the ideas of Mani, which contributed to Augustine's doctrine of original sin. Manichaeism taught that Satan attacked the earth and defeated humans sent against him by the God of light, but he was overthrown by God, who then created Adam and Eve.[4]

> To what extent does Christian tradition influence your view of the relationship between God and Satan? What challenges you or makes you want to know more? How can these traditional views be helpful or hurtful in our faith journey?

Belief in Satan rose to new heights in the Middle Ages, when Christians saw themselves to be in continuous conflict with him. This pessimistic view influenced Luther, who spoke of being constantly aware of the presence and antagonism of a supernatural adversary. For him, the devil was always around, practicing his wily schemes and cunning entrapments and making the achievement of a better world an impossibility.[5] The practice of the early fathers to attribute dissenting views to Satan led later generations to demonize Jews, pagans, and other Christians as heretics worthy of excommunication, torture, and death. In more recent times, however, with the advent of scientific thinking, belief in Satan and demons has ceased to be an essential element of Christian belief. Still, the ongoing experience of believers testifies to a larger-than-life evil influence affecting behavior and events, as we have seen in the chapter on temptation.

The Devil: A Fallen Angel

A long tradition sees Satan as more than just a symbol of our human impulses of lust, anger, greed, and hostility. Instead, he is conceived as an evil spirit or power that shapes human behavior and events. Originally, the tradition states, he was one of God's angels, a member in good standing of the heavenly court, a messenger doing God's bidding on earth. Sometimes named Lucifer, he rebelled against God, fell under God's judgment, and was banished to a nether realm, often called hell. Thenceforth he continued his open revolt against God and all things good, enticing humans to join him in his rebellion and causing untold havoc on earth. Some identify him with certain historical persons or movements in history: Nebuchadnezzar, Caesar, Hitler, Stalin, or an "axis of evil."

Others, like Walter Wink in his book *The Powers That Be*, speak of a palpable spiritual force at the core of political, economic, military, and cultural institutions—both in biblical times and today—a "domination system" that powerfully shapes its members and influences the course of events.[6] This is the principalities and powers mentioned in Ephesians 6:12 (KJV), a formative ethos that seems overwhelming in its power and undermines the human values of freedom, dignity, justice, and personal worth. This domination system is the form taken by Satan in our time. Nations and institutions that began with high ideals and noble purposes and believed themselves chosen by God to achieve good things have "fallen from grace," like Lucifer of old. Corrupted by a spirit of evil that besieges from without and gnaws from within, they lose their way, corrupt their leaders with delusions of grandeur and the craving of greed, exploit their members (employees, citizens, customers, stockholders), and contaminate everything they touch (natural environment, systems of law, education, health care, business, international affairs). The fall—whether of Adam and Eve, the biblical first humans; Lucifer, the good angel turned rebel; or the benign principalities and powers morphed into domination systems— seems to be a universal experience.

> Why does the theme of "the fall" appear so widely in mythology, Scripture, history, and socio-political analysis? How do we respond to the idea that the "domination system" is the form taken by Satan in our time? What aspects of this system have we observed? What examples of the fall have we seen in our lifetime? In our church? In our own lives?

"All Things Under His Feet"

Devastating experiences like those faced by Hank, the World War II GI (and participants/victims in every war); Elie Wiesel in a death camp; and the West family in their living room can cause us to feel that God is dead and Satan has been enthroned. But the Bible tells us otherwise. The writer of Ephesians exclaims, "God put this power to work in Christ when he raised him from the dead and seated him at his right hand..., far above all rule and authority and power and dominion, and above every name that is named.... And he has put all things under his feet and has made him the head over all things for the church" (1:20-22).

The signs of the times celebrate Satan's rule, but through the eyes of faith, we see another reality. By the power of the Almighty, the risen Christ has stomped on the serpent, claimed authority over all things, charted a new course for human destiny, and called the church to proclaim the good news of Christ's eternal reign. "Thanks be to God, who gives us the victory through our Lord Jesus Christ" (1 Corinthians 15:57)!

Closing Prayer
Sing "Thine Be the Glory" or "All Hail the Power of Jesus' Name." Close with the unison benediction "May the God of hope fill you with all joy and peace in believing, so that you may abound in hope by the power of the Holy Spirit" (Romans 15:13).

Notes

[1] From *Dear God! (If There Is a God . . .): The Collected Writings of Harry Zeitlin,* edited by Stephen Wing and Dawn Aura (Ariel Press, 2004); pages 15, 30.

[2] From *Night,* by Elie Wiesel (Avon Books, 1960); pages 75–76.

[3] See *The Encyclopedia Britannica*, 14th edition, Vol. 7 (Encyclopedia Britannica, 1929); page 293. Also see *The Old Enemy: Satan and the Combat Myth,* by Neil Forsyth (Princeton University Press, 1987); pages 5, 207, 392. Note that there are variations in the spelling of several of these personifications.

[4] See *The Oxford Dictionary of the Christian Church* (Oxford University Press, 1983) for more information about Gnosticism, Marcionism, Manichaeism, and Pelagianism. Also see *The Old Enemy: Satan and the Combat Myth*; pages 309–440.

[5] See *The Origin of Satan,* by Elaine Pagels (Random House, 1995); pages 158, 180. Also see *The Old Enemy: Satan and the Combat Myth*; pages 3, 7, 439.

[6] See *The Powers That Be: Theology for a New Millennium,* by Walter Wink (Doubleday, 1998); pages 37–62.

CHAPTER 4
DEMON POSSESSION AND EXORCISM

Who can calm the troubled spirit?

Focus: This chapter relates the experience of demon possession and exorcism in biblical times and traditional societies to contemporary forms of mental illness and healing.

Gathering

Begin by "checking in" with each other. How have things gone this week? What concerns are you facing in the days to come—health issues, important decisions, family situations, spiritual concerns, current events? What prayer requests do you have? Spend time in prayer for these concerns. Then sing "Spirit of the Living God."

The "Bipolar" Evil Spirit

As a small boy, Malcolm was loud, hyperactive, and mischievous. Later he was diagnosed with attention deficit disorder (ADD). As a teenager, he got poor grades, started drinking and taking drugs, and got in trouble with the police for petty thievery. He barely finished high school. College was out of the question. His parents were at their wits' end to know how to deal with him. His father tended to be lenient, while his mother tried to discipline his erratic behavior. Frustration and arguments over how to deal with Malcolm played a part in their deteriorating relationship, and eventually they were divorced. In his early twenties,

Malcolm became a full-fledged alcoholic, moved back and forth between his parents, opened a drug paraphernalia store, got shot by an enraged customer, and was in and out of jail on drug-related charges.

How do you understand Malcolm's bipolar condition and attention deficit disorder? What other factors might be involved in his circumstances? What connections do you make between his condition and being possessed with an evil spirit?

Finally, kicked out of both homes, he left town, and for long stretches neither parent knew where he was. When he came back penniless, his mother took him in on the condition that he would seek psychiatric help. Several times he went through detox treatment, stayed sober awhile, then fell off the wagon. Finally, one doctor diagnosed him as bipolar (manic-depressive) and put him on medication. This worked for a while, but he would forget or refuse to take his meds, and the cycle would begin all over again. Now in his early thirties, Malcolm is broke, unemployed, living with his mother, and has no motivation to do anything with his life except live day to day. He is possessed with an "evil spirit" that has destroyed his life, taken away any sense of meaning or purpose, and disturbed the lives of all who seek to love and help him.

Exorcism in the "Power House"

Daniel Ling is a pastor in upstate New York who grew up in a small Malaysian village with no electricity, running water, or paved roads. His boyhood experience with demon possession was very different from Malcolm's. He described it to me in a letter:

> There was a "power house" connected to our church, called the "prayer house." Every morning dedicated Christians would gather to pray and study the Scriptures. It was a well-known fact that these prayer partners could do exorcism. A demon-possessed person was referred by either family members or church leaders. The prayer leader would interview the possessed person and his family regarding the symptoms, some of which were sleeplessness, disturbing others, getting violent, destroying property, hearing voices, talking nonsense, terrible headaches, and general dysfunctional behavior.
>
> Members of the prayer group would gather around the possessed person and pray aloud simultaneously, then take turns asking questions such as:

Who are you? Why are you possessing this person? After another round of loud simultaneous prayer, the group would take hold of the person's hands and feet and the leader would say, "In the name of Jesus, I command you to come out of this person!" Then there would be lots of struggle, kicking, screaming, threatening, bargaining, making false promises, foaming, spitting, cursing, and other violent behavior.

The prayer partners had to hold on tightly to the hands and feet and force the devil to leave through the head. Once the devil surrendered, all resistance would subside and the person would fall into a deep sleep. Awaking, they would act like a new creation. Testimonies would follow, and many were added to the fold. I do not doubt the faith of this prayer group. They were sincere and powerful, by the grace of God. I have seen what the devil can do to a person. In that environment and during those times, it was very real and vivid for me. I was only 13 years old.[1]

We could say that bipolar Malcolm and the demon-possessed Chinese peasants of Daniel Ling's childhood were Satan-afflicted persons. Whether such spiritual maladies are given a medical diagnosis or not, the effect on the victim is similar: mental disturbance, inability to function, disoriented life, alienation from loved ones, separation from God and self, and overall misery. The "spirit" that dominates such persons is clearly evil. Only God has power over it. And human agents—whether through therapy, medication, or prayer—can draw on the loving power of God to dispel it.

> How do you respond to Daniel Ling's boyhood memory of the healing of those who were demon possessed? Do you think they had some form of mental illness or something entirely different? Why? Do you think demons are real beings or personifications of mental agitation? Are the mental, emotional, and spiritual different aspects of our being or different words for the same reality? How do you understand exorcism? What connections, if any, do you see between exorcism and the healing performed by doctors? What is the place of prayer in healing?

Jesus Casts Out Evil Spirits

Let us now examine the instances of Jesus' encounters with demons and healings of the demon possessed—mighty works demonstrating Jesus' power and authority as one come from God. The first occurs in the synagogue in Capernaum (Mark 1:21-28; see also Luke 4:33-37). Jesus has been teaching "as one having authority, and not as the scribes." Suddenly a man accosts him, identifying him as "the Holy One of God" and demanding to know why he has come to trouble them. Realizing that this crude behavior does not reflect the man's true nature, Jesus orders the "unclean spirit" to leave him. After a noisy seizure, the man becomes calm, the onlookers are dumbfounded, Jesus' authority is enhanced, and his renown is extended farther afield. A man's life has been turned around, new believers have been won, and God has been glorified.

Next, in his first venture into Gentile territory, where pigs could be raised, Jesus once again enters into conflict with the power of evil by exorcising the Gerasene demoniac who lived in caves in the wilds (Mark 5:1-20; see also Matthew 8:28-34 and Luke 8:26-39; see the reference in Isaiah 65:4-5 to persons who "sit inside tombs, / and…eat swine's flesh," whom God commanded, "Do not come near me, for I am too holy for you"). Usually, exorcisms involved the encounter with the demoniac, the silencing of the demon, its expulsion and departure, and the response of the crowd. But here the order is different. On sighting Jesus from afar, the demoniac runs up, falls down, worships him as "Son of the Most High God," and urges him in God's name not to bother him. But Jesus orders the demon to leave, then asks his name. The man's response, "Legion," refers to a large Roman army unit of 4,000 to 6,000 men, suggesting a malady of multiple identities. In response to the demons' request not to be banished from the area, Jesus allows them to invade a herd of pigs that, thus tormented, run in a frenzy over a cliff to be drowned in the Sea of Galilee.

> Read the story of the healing in the synagogue in Capernaum in Mark 1:21-28 (Luke 4:33-37) and the story of Gerasene demoniac in Mark 5:1-20 (Matthew 8:28-34; Luke 8:26-39). What connections do you see between the healing and the authority and power of Jesus? How do the stories demonstrate compassion? How do they demonstrate fear? What connections do you see between these healing stories and the stories of Malcolm and Daniel Ling at the beginning of the session?

Frightened by such bizarre happenings—and no doubt angry at this sudden loss of their livestock—the herdsmen run back into the town of

Gerasa, loudly reporting along the way what this wonder worker Jesus has done. Soon a crowd of townspeople assembles and sees the formerly disturbed man fully dressed and acting normal. When the story is confirmed by eyewitnesses, they grow frightened and awestruck, imploring Jesus to leave. True, one person has been restored to sanity, but the livelihood of several has been destroyed, and they don't want their area getting a reputation for weird goings-on. So Jesus obliges by descending the hill to his boat. Knowing he had been ostracized for his strange behavior and sensing he still might be rejected because of the mysterious way he was healed, the man follows Jesus and begs to go with him. But Jesus says, "Go home to your friends, and tell them how much the Lord has done for you." So the man becomes a missionary to all the Decapolis (a federation of ten Gentile cities in eastern Palestine). A man with a split-personality disorder (schizophrenia?) has been restored to wholeness. The ensuing furor stampedes a herd of pigs to their deaths. Bystanders become both terrified and irate. In spite of the good he has done, the Healer becomes persona non grata. The healed man is transformed into a witness for God. The evil spirits are replaced by the Spirit of God.

Reflecting the worldview of their time, the Gospel writers also attribute blindness and the inability to speak to demon possession. Miracle stories describing Jesus as casting out this kind of demon are found in Matthew 9:32-34 (see also Luke 11:14-15) and 12:22-32. In the first incident, persons (friends? family? village elders?) bring the mute to Jesus, Jesus expels the demon, and the person is able to speak. The onlookers are astounded by the uniqueness of the event, but the religious leaders—perhaps threatened by an unknown who demonstrates a potency they do not possess—attribute Jesus' mysterious power to Satan ("ruler of the demons") rather than God.

In the second event in Matthew 12, differing from the first only in that the victim is both blind and mute, Jesus empowers the demoniac to see and speak, and the "ruler of demons" is given the

> Read Matthew 9:32-34 (Luke 11:14-15) and Matthew 12:22-32. Review the effects of the healing on the victims, the bystanders, and the critics among the Pharisees. What do these reactions say to you? Why do you think the critics of Jesus attributed his healing power to the "ruler of the demons"? How do these stories compare to those of Malcolm and Daniel Ling at the beginning of the session?

49

legendary name Beelzebul (originally meaning "prince of the Canaanite god Baal" but in Jesus' time applied to Satan).[2] Jesus contests the insult, arguing that it would be self-defeating for Satan to do good works and throwing the question back at his accusers by asking upon whose power their own exorcists draw. Using the analogy of a thief having to tie up a householder before he can carry out his robbery, Jesus implies that in order to cast out demons, he first has to shackle the devil and render him powerless. To say "whoever is not with me is against me" is tantamount to accusing his critics of working against God. By calling God Satan, they are blaspheming (showing contempt for the Holy), which is the unpardonable sin.

In these stories, not only mental but also physical disorders are attributed to demons. Also, demon possession is seen as the work of the devil. Jesus shows his concern for the hurting and his ability to heal both mind and body, while his enemies seek to discredit him by claiming his power comes from Satan, not God. Jesus stands up to his accusers with both logic and spiritual integrity.

> Read Mark 7:24-30 (Matthew 15:21-28). What do you make of Jesus' initial reaction to the Syrophoenician woman? What does the healing say to you about Jesus' power? What can we learn from this story to strengthen our own faith and discipleship? What connections do you see between this story and those of Malcolm and Daniel Ling?

In Mark 7:24-30 (see also Matthew 15:21-28), Jesus is again in Gentile territory (Tyre and Sidon—present-day Lebanon). He seeks seclusion, but his privacy is disturbed by a Syrophoenician woman whose daughter is demon possessed (symptoms not described). In what seems like an ill-considered effort to get rid of the woman, Jesus humiliates her by comparing her to a dog that doesn't deserve to sit at the table with a Jew. But, motivated by her concern for the health of her daughter, she takes the insult in stride and persists by begging for the "crumbs" of his love and healing power. Impressed with her faith, Jesus responds to her request and in absentia restores her daughter to her right mind. When the woman returns home, she finds a normal girl lying on her bed. Here Jesus—albeit reluctantly—employs God's healing power in response to the faith of a Gentile woman to neutralize Satan's influence over the mind of a little girl some distance away. Apparently, exorcism does not require physical touch or presence, is not limited to members of any particular religion, and is related to faith and intercessory prayer.

In Matthew 17:14-21 (see also Mark 9:14-29 and Luke 9:37-42), demon possession is equated with epilepsy. The victim is described as stiffening, becoming speechless, foaming, grinding his teeth (Mark), shrieking and convulsing (Luke), falling into both fire and water, and suffering greatly (Matthew). Jesus, Peter, James, and John have just descended from a mountaintop experience. Approaching the other disciples, they see a large crowd gathered, listening to an argument with some religious leaders. The boy's father has sought healing from the disciples, but they are unable to help, a failure that exasperates Jesus. He deplores the lack of faith in them and all his contemporaries. In desperation, the man kneels before Jesus and begs for help. When the lad is brought to Jesus, he is seized with an epileptic fit, falls to the ground, and foams at the mouth. Jesus asks how long he has been affected this way, and the father replies since childhood. In Mark's version, the father prefaces his request for his son's healing with "if you are able

> Read Matthew 17:14-21. What challenges you about this story of exorcism? What role, if any, do you think faith, prayer, and fasting have in healing? What do you think or feel about the notion that a person is not healed because he or she has inadequate faith?

to do anything," to which Jesus replies, "All things can be done for the one who believes." In response, the man expresses his ambivalence in the oft-quoted statement "I believe; help my unbelief!" Jesus then reprimands the demon for blocking the boy's speech and hearing, then orders it to leave him and never return. In a final, violent convulsion, the evil spirit departs, and the boy falls into a coma, causing bystanders to think him dead. But Jesus draws him to his feet, and the boy stands erect—restored to health and wholeness. When the disciples ask why their efforts had failed, Jesus points to their lack of faith and stresses the need for prayer and fasting in preparation for such an exorcism. Here, once again, faith and prayer appear as essentials in doing battle with the forces of Satan that bind persons with physical and spiritual restraints, preventing them from being all God intends them to be.

In Luke 8:2-3, a final reference speaks of a group of women accompanying and supporting Jesus and the twelve, including Joanna of Herod's court, Susanna, and others who had been "cured of evil spirits and infirmities." Of special note is "Mary, called Magdalene, from whom seven demons had gone out." We can only speculate as to what these seven spirits might have been—perhaps poverty, ostracism, disease, loneliness, self-rejection, depression, and remorse. To be sure, affliction by seven demons was a worse condition than being possessed by only one. Jesus makes this point in Luke 11:24-26 when speaking about the state of a person who, freed from domination by an evil spirit, fails to invite God's Spirit in to fill the vacancy.

> What do you think it means to "invite God's Spirit in to fill the vacancy" when a person has been freed from domination by an evil spirit?

Lacking the resilience to withstand evil influence, the empty heart is then filled by a host of bad spirits, and one's spiritual condition goes from bad to worse. In these verses, we see Jesus' concern for bringing wholeness to women marginalized by a patriarchal society and for including them in his inner circle. We are also made aware of the importance of inviting the spirit of goodness into one's life to fill the void left by the conquest of sin and the rejection of bad attitudes, feelings, and behavior.

Early Followers of Jesus Cast Out Evil Spirits

Evil spirits and their expulsion also played an important part in the ministry of the apostles in the years after Jesus' death and resurrection. In Acts 5:12-16, we read that "many signs and wonders were done among the people through the apostles," with people bringing the sick and "those tormented by unclean spirits, and they were all cured." Acts 8:4-8 describes how Philip preached Christ in Samaria and brought joy and deliverance to the people through the healings he performed. The lame were cured, and "unclean spirits, crying with loud shrieks, came out of many who were possessed."

In Ephesus, Paul and Silas met a slave girl with "a spirit of divination" who followed and harassed them (Acts 16:16 and following). Finally, Paul confronted the spirit, saying, "I order you in the name of Jesus Christ to come out of her." The girl was restored to her right mind, much to the consternation of her owners, who were profiting from her sorcery. On a later visit to Ephesus, Paul again cast out evil spirits (Acts 19:11-20), but this time other Jewish magicians tried to imitate him by exorcising demons in the name of

Jesus. The demons didn't recognize them, however, and attacked and drove them away. The residents were impressed, praised Jesus, and became believers. The magicians burned their books and gave up their nefarious practices, and "the word of the Lord grew mightily and prevailed."

Reference to evil spirits is also made in the epistles: "For our struggle is not against enemies of blood and flesh, but against…the spiritual forces of evil in the heavenly places" (Ephesians 6:12). The writer of First Timothy speaks of "deceitful spirits and teachings of demons" who seduce the faithful with heretical doctrines (4:1). And James 2:19 tells of demons who "believe—and shudder," suggesting that the fallen angels knew the truth and trembled before God's power even as they sought to defy it.

> Read Acts 8:4-8, Acts 16:16 and following, Acts 19:11-20, Ephesians 6:12, 1 Timothy 4:1, and James 2:19. Identify the beliefs about evil spirits in the New Testament worldview, the effects of the Christian gospel on those afflicted by them, and the influence of the ministry of exorcism on those who observed the apostles practicing it. What in our lives and faith corresponds to this New Testament worldview? In what ways have our spirits been plagued by evil forces? How can we draw on the power of Christ (love) to overcome the evils that beset us?

Clearly, the early Christians were no strangers to evil forces in their world. They saw their effects in the bodies and souls of those about them, utilized the power of Christ to defeat them and their practitioners, and won many to Christ through the ministry of spiritual exorcism.

Closing Prayer

List the "evil spirits" that infect our lives and separate us from God—attitudes of jealousy, envy, antagonism, desire, rage; physical maladies such as cancer, heart disease, obesity, diabetes, asthma; emotional disorders like stress, depression, anxiety, fear; conditions handicapping sight, hearing, movement, speech; and spiritual states such as self-centeredness, alienation, despair, greed. Recall the range of demon-possessed conditions that Jesus exorcised.

Choose one or both of the prayer experiences below:

1. Pray for healing with the laying on of hands. If you are comfortable with this traditional form of prayer, take turns sitting or standing in the center of a prayer circle. Gently place hands on the shoulders, back, or head of the person in the center. Ask God, through Jesus, to cast out the "evil spirits," to heal the person in the center, or to address a specific need named by the one who is in the center.

2. Pray aloud the following prayer: "God of all that is good, we pray in the name of Jesus for your gifts of healing and wholeness for all who are here, for our nation, and for all creation. We pray as Jesus taught us to pray: (pray the Lord's Prayer)."

Close by singing "Here I am, Lord" or "There Is a Balm in Gilead."

Notes

[1] From a letter to the writer; used by permission.

[2] See the note related to Matthew 12:24 in *The New Oxford Annotated Bible* (Oxford University Press, 2001). Over time it may also have had the pejorative meanings "lord of the flies" and "lord of dung." See *Harper's Bible Dictionary* (HarperSanFrancisco, 1985); page 100.

CHAPTER 5
THE ANTICHRIST
AND THE END TIMES

What does the future hold,
and who holds the future?

Focus: This chapter explores biblical perspectives on the antichrist in relation to Satan, exchatology (end-times beliefs), the Second Coming, and Christian hope.

Gathering
Begin by discussing:

- What are our hopes for the future? Which of these are personal or family aspirations? Dreams for a better world? Spiritual desires? On what do we base these?
- Are we optimistic about the future? Hopeful? Why or why not? What is the difference between optimism and hope?

Sing the hymn "Hope of the World."

Who Is the Antichrist?

The aspect of end-times teaching that relates especially to our study of Satan is that of the antichrist, who is mentioned by name only four times in the entire Bible—all in the letters of John. These references are as follows:

- "Children, it is the last hour! As you have heard that antichrist is coming, so now many antichrists have come. From this we know that it is the last hour" (1 John 2:18).

- "Who is the liar but the one who denies that Jesus is the Christ? This is the antichrist, the one who denies the Father and the Son" (1 John 2:22).
- "Every spirit that does not confess Jesus is not from God. And this is the spirit of the antichrist, of which you have heard that it is coming; and now it is already in the world" (1 John 4:3).
- "Many deceivers have gone out into the world, those who do not confess that Jesus Christ has come in the flesh; any such person is the deceiver and the antichrist!" (2 John 7).

Read the Scriptures mentioned in this section and discuss:

- Who did New Testament writers believe to be the antichrist? What are his characteristics? Is he the same as or different from Satan? Is he to be identified with an historical figure in New Testament times? In every time? In our time? In the end times? Or is he a non-personal force that seeks to shape persons and history in evil ways?
- What present-day phenomena might be attributed to the influence of an antichrist? How can we cooperate with God to oppose the power of the antichrist? What gives us hope in the face of any apparent domination of the world by the antichrist?

From these verses, we may conclude that: 1) the end times seemed imminent to John, who wrote at the end of the first century A.D.; 2) there were many antichrists, not just one; 3) they were schismatics (probably Gnostics), false teachers who had left the church and were disturbing the faith of believers; 4) they were not godly; and 5) they were called liars or deceivers because they denied that Jesus was fully human. Any heretic (person who chooses beliefs contrary to accepted orthodoxy) may be labeled *antichrist*—that is, "against Christ" or opposed to the importance of the incarnation.

John sees the coming of the antichrist as the fulfillment of an earlier prophecy, probably Jesus' mention in Mark 13:14 and Matthew 24:15 of a "desolating sacrilege standing in the holy place"—i.e., a human being claiming divine worship. Without using the term *antichrist,* Paul mentions in 2 Thessalonians 2:3-4 the "lawless one . . . [who] opposes and exalts himself above every so-called god or object of worship, so that he takes his seat in the temple of God, declaring himself to be God," an allusion to this same saying of Jesus.

In the Book of Revelation, the antichrist is called the "beast" who arises from the bottomless pit or sea (11:7; 13:1) and symbolizes the powers that persecute the church (13:7). He is given the features of the antichrist: he looks deceptively like a lamb (i.e., Christ; 13:11), speaks like a dragon (i.e., an evil ruler; 13:15), is accompanied by a false prophet (16:13; 19:20; 20:10), and organizes the nations for the final battle against God at Armageddon (16:16). Together, the beast and the false prophet deceive people (13:14; 19:20) and are identified with Rome (the "seven mountains" of 17:9) and more widely with all earthly governments who demand allegiance to purposes contrary to God's will. In the Middle Ages, Pope Innocent III designated Mohammed as the antichrist. Later, the Reformers called the papal church the antichrist. More recent interpreters have variously identified the antichrist with Hitler, the Pope, the Soviet empire, Saddam Hussein, and the Nation of Islam.

It can thus be concluded that the redemptive work of Christ and his church was bitterly opposed by Satan. His hostility would reach its climax when by his power he would enable a person or body to appear like Christ, pretending to do good and bring ultimate redemption when actually his aim was to undercut Christ's work. So great would be the cunning of the antichrist (Satan) that some Christians would be seduced into forsaking the true faith and would follow him instead. This would bring history to an end and would be followed by Christ's return for judgment.

Victory Over Evil

Various points of view regarding the end of time offer the hope of ultimate victory over the antichrist and evil, which is the overarching theme of apocalyptic thought that informs much writing in the New Testament. God's justice, mercy, and love will overcome all evil. The works of fiction in the Left Behind Series are based upon a particular viewpoint about what is expected to happen during the last days. In this point of view, an antichrist will rule.

Left Behind

The first volume in the popular Left Behind Series of novels begins with the Rapture—the sudden snatching up of millions of the faithful into heaven. Subsequent books follow the adventures of a small band of those left behind on earth through the seven-year tribulation and rule of the antichrist. They have now become believers and are fighting to stay alive as they engage the antichrist and his followers, who rule the world. They are guided by a videotape left behind to give instructions for life after the rapture of all the saved, which expounds Scriptures like 1 Corinthians 15 and the Book of Revelation from a futurist, premillennial, dispensationalist viewpoint to show what to expect in the years to come. From this perspective, the seven years after the Rapture will be a period of tribulation that will bring, in order, the seven Seal Judgments, the seven Trumpet Judgments, and the seven Vial Judgments—the Great Tribulation. At the end of this, the faithful will be rewarded by seeing the "Glorious Appearing" of Christ returning to set up his thousand-year reign on earth—the Millennium.

During the tribulation (see Revelation 7:14, KJV), the antichrist will come to power, promising peace and trying to unite the world. He will be a great deceiver, and when his true goals are revealed, he will be opposed. This will result in a great war—the Battle of Armageddon (so named because it will take place on the plain of Megiddo in northern Israel). The twelfth and final installment in the Left Behind Series, *Glorious Appearing,* graphically describes the return of Jesus, the Battle of Armageddon, and the Last Judgment, with non-Christians gathered to Jesus' left, their bodies ripped open, then tossed into everlasting fire, howling and screeching in agony. This view of a demonic but historical antichrist, a violent Armageddon, and a bloody Second Coming projects a view of the future in which wars and other calamities will continue to worsen until God raises a righteous elite up to heaven to watch the "left behind" endure even more torment—all in realization of biblical prophecy. It welcomes armed conflict, interpreted to fulfill ancient predictions about the struggle between good and evil, and sees current events as the inevitable playing out of God's plan for the end of history. It also reflects a shift in portrayals of Jesus from a gentle, compassionate figure to a militant Messiah presiding over a sea of blood. Thus, the Left Behind novels and the futurist, dispensationalist, premillennial interpretation of the Bible that they reflect project an extremely pessimistic view of history.[1]

> Do you agree or disagree with the assertion that the futuristic, dispensationalist, premillennial interpretation of the Bible reflected in the Left Behind Series projects an extremely pessimistic view of history? Why?

The word *futurist* is meant to focus on future events in preference to present realities and past heritage. *Dispensational* suggests God relates to humankind via different covenants (dispensations); in particular, dispensationalists believe that God's covenant with Israel, including promises of land, continues in full force distinct from Christianity. *Millennial* refers to the belief that Christ will have a thousand-year earthly reign of peace—or millennium—before the Last Judgment. *Premillennial* means that Christ will return prior to a literal end-times millennium to lead his armies at Armageddon.

This view of the Rapture, antichrist, tribulation, and Armageddon leads to the view that the unfolding of wars and tragedies are evidence pointing to the Second Coming. The establishment of the state of Israel, hoped-for rebuilding of a third temple, rise of the antichrist, and buildup of armies poised to attack Israel are among the signs leading to the final battle and Jesus' return. Current political developments are viewed in light of a prophetic schedule of events that should unfold according to this view of Scripture. The escalating power and influence of satanic forces aligned to the antichrist who will battle Israel are signs that the end is drawing near. Judgment will befall nations and individuals according to how they bless Israel (Genesis 12:3). After the godless forces opposed to both God and Israel are defeated at Armageddon, Jesus will reign as a Jewish Messiah in Jerusalem for a thousand years, and the Jewish people who have accepted Christ will enjoy a privileged status and role in the world.

> What thoughts or feelings do you have about the view of the end times portrayed in the Left Behind series? What parallels do you see, if any, between current events and accounts in the Book of Revelation and other apocalyptic writings? Are you pessimistic or optimistic about the future? What gives us hope?

Millennial Dispensationalism Assessed

The futurist, dispensationalist, and premillennial interpretations of Scripture, which were popularized by the notes of the *Scofield Reference Bible*, teach that the last days of history are signaled by dramatic events that will lead to the sudden return of Jesus. Prior to this, the world will be threatened by evil forces that will culminate in the rise of one demonic world leader: the antichrist. Once Israel became a nation in 1948, the movement toward the last days was set in motion. Israel (the modern state is equated with biblical Israel) was God's chosen instrument to fight the antichrist. Jesus will return to save Israel and establish his millennial kingdom in that land. Born-again Christians will be raptured and will not pass through the years of tribulation.

Those reading Scripture from more historical and analytical perspectives offer the following critiques of premillennial dispensationalism:

(1) It projects into the future Old and New Testament promises that were actually addressed to current situations in biblical times. For example, Jesus spoke of the scattering and latter-day regathering of the Jewish people (Luke 21:23-24, 28), which the modern-day restoration of Israel fulfills. But these verses say nothing about Israel's reoccupation of the land. Instead, they point to Rome's destruction of Jerusalem, an event that took place in 66–70 A.D. and thus was already fulfilled by the time Luke wrote his Gospel.

(2) This "apocalyptic" (revelatory of a cataclysmic end) interpretation was popular in Jesus' time. It was a primary belief of the Qumran community living along the Dead Sea, which anticipated a future restoration of the Jewish people in the holy land. This view is reflected in Acts 1:6-9, where the disciples ask Jesus, "Is this the time when you will restore the kingdom to Israel?" Jesus replies that God's times are not for them to know; rather, they are to trust the God of history and live the gospel of the kingdom now. To this end, they would receive the power of the Holy Spirit and become witnesses both locally and globally (1:8). Thus, the risen Lord counseled against waiting for an end-times fulfillment of biblical promises and instead urged commitment to the Spirit-led mission in the present.

Pair up and discuss the differences between the end-times views of dispensationalists and their critics, one posing the claims of the former and the other countering with views of the latter. Come together as a total group and discuss:

- What are the strengths of each position? The shortcomings?
- What is important about each? What does each contribute to Christian hope?
- What does each offer in the way of nurture of our faith and discipleship?

---

(3) Dispensationalism is oriented more to the Abrahamic covenant than to the cross and is centered more on the Jewish kingdom than on the body of Christ. It interprets the New Testament in light of Old Testament prophecies rather than viewing the Old in light of the revelation of Jesus Christ in the New. Further, it identifies the Christian gospel with an ideology of political success and military conquest in ways contrary to the central teachings of the Prince of Peace.[2]

Jesus' Teaching About the End Times

In response to the apocalyptic views of the Essenes in Qumran, the questions of his disciples, and the speculations of generations of Christians since, Jesus offers the following guidance for our thinking about the future:

(1) No human—not even Jesus himself—knows when the end will come. In Mark 13:32, he says, "But about that day or hour no one knows, neither the angels in heaven, nor the Son, but only the Father." And in Acts 1:7, he tells his disciples, "It is not for you to know the times or periods that the Father has set by his own authority."

(2) Satan has fallen; he is no longer reigning. Jesus said, "I watched Satan fall from heaven like a flash of lightning…. I have given you authority…over all the power of the enemy" (Luke 10:18-19). Now is the time to celebrate, not to mourn (Mark 2:18-20), because the victory over evil has already been won. Satan has been defeated. God's reign has come, God's power is available to us, and God's promise has been fulfilled in Christ. The teaching that the world is still under the devil's control or that the reign of Satan still lies in the future has some scriptural support (e.g., Revelation 20:7-10), but it contradicts this vision of Jesus in which Satan has already fallen.

(3) God does not play favorites. "Many who are first will be last, and the last will be first" (Matthew 19:30). The poor, blind, captives, and oppressed will be blessed in the "year of the Lord's favor," while the self-righteous who wait for God's vengeance on their enemies will be disappointed (Luke 4:16-19). In Christ's coming reign, both the righteous who expect to be blessed and the outcasts who have given up hope are in for a surprise. This may upset some people; it angered the citizens of Nazareth, who attempted to throw Jesus off the cliff (Luke 4:28-29). Nonetheless, the Christ who is to come will cause the high to be brought low and the lowly to be elevated (Luke 14:11).

(4) No signs will help us know when the end is near. "Truly I tell you, no sign will be given to this generation" (Mark 8:12). Jesus repudiated the fortunetelling and sign-reading tendencies in the popular religion of his and every age. We may be able to use signs to predict the weather, but none will be given for the last days "except the sign of Jonah" (Matthew 16:1-4). The sign of Jonah refers to the death and resurrection of Jesus (Matthew 12:39-40). It demonstrates the power of God's love to convert and save sinners. It shows what God intends to do for all people: save them.

Read the Scripture passages referred to in the section "Jesus' Teaching About the End Times." Put the main point of each into a single sentence. What does each suggest about hope for the future? How does each inform our expression of Christian faith and discipleship?

(5) Those who think they are on God's side may be disappointed. Jesus referred to the religious leaders of his day as a "brood of vipers" who may not "escape being sentenced to hell" (Matthew 23:29-39). To assume that we are the ones to be vindicated in Christ's coming reign while those who oppose us are condemned is to exhibit the same kind of self-righteousness Jesus was criticizing. Rather than taking a vindictive attitude and looking for God to punish our enemies, the more appropriate attitude is that of Jesus. He had compassion on Jerusalem, the wicked city, and wanted to gather its "children together as a hen gathers her brood under her wings" (Matthew 23:37).

(6) In the Last Supper, Jesus uses the bread and cup to symbolize that his broken body and shed blood would be offered to bring about the reconciliation of all to God and one another. Jesus' teachings and ministry also emphasize the joyous celebration and loving reconciliation of the messianic banquet. In response to the centurion's faith, Jesus comments, "I tell you, many will come from east and west and will eat with Abraham and Isaac and Jacob in the kingdom" (Matthew 8:11). The last days will be a time for rejoicing as God unites all peoples in a glorious meal of peace and celebration. Jesus scandalized people by beginning the feasting and reconciliation in his lifetime. "The Son of Man came eating and drinking" (Matthew 11:16-19). His was a different kind of reign. He would proclaim forgiveness now so sinners could share in the table fellowship of the redemptive community and begin celebrating the new age.

Jesus saw the coming age as a time for reconciliation, fellowship, joy, and celebration.

Jesus calls us to love one another and proclaim the gospel of love and justice. When asked if he would restore the kingdom to Israel, he told his disciples not to worry about times or periods, which were God's business. Instead, "you will receive power when the Holy Spirit has come upon you; and you will be my witnesses in Jerusalem, in all Judea and Samaria, and to the ends of the earth" (Acts 1:6-8). He told them to learn to live the new life of discipleship, going into the difficult places of persecution and crucifixion and living out the gospel—even when it brought opposition. Then he vanished from sight, without having answered their questions about the future but instead leaving them the task of living as servants of the living God in the here and now.

Hope in Christ for All Time

Whether you agree or disagree with the end-times teachings explored in this session, a common thread to all such perspectives is God's triumph over evil through Christ. We can have confidence in the power of God to overcome the wiles of the antichrist both within and beyond history. We can live in the assurance that regardless of what the future holds, God holds the future.

Closing Prayer

Review the sources of hope mentioned in this chapter: promises to the faithful in the Left Behind literature, Jesus' exhortation not to worry about the future but rather to accept empowerment by the Spirit for loving witness in the present, and joyful anticipation of an inclusive meal of celebration in the age to come. What is your response to these sources of hope?

Close by singing "A Mighty Fortress Is Our God" and praying for strength and guidance in the struggle against the antichrist in both our individual lives and the social and political structures of power.

Notes

[1] See *Anxious for Armageddon,* by Donald E.Wagner (Herald Press, 1995). This book deals with millennial dispensationalism but not the Left Behind novels. After reading the first novel and descriptions of the others in the Left Behind Series, I gave a book review of Wagner's book. I incorporated that review into this session.

[2] See *Anxious for Armageddon.* Also see *Jesus Against the Rapture: Seven Unexpected Prophecies,* by Robert Jewett (The Westminster Press, 1979).

CHAPTER 6
THE DEVIL IN "THE OTHER"
—AND IN US

Who is to blame?

Focus: In this chapter, we confront the human tendency to project evil onto "the other" and the need to acknowledge its presence within us.

Gathering

After greeting one another, stand in the middle of the room. If you agree with the statements below, move to the right. If you disagree, move to the left. No one may remain in the middle; all must choose one option or the other.

1. Our enemies are evil; we are good.
2. When I make a decision, I'm sure I'm right.
3. In an argument, I try to listen to the other side before stating my case.
4. I often feel sinful and unworthy.
5. I usually feel pretty good about myself.
6. I'm easily influenced by others.
7. I always stand firm for what I believe.
8. In my decisions, I pray and follow God's leading.
9. In my decisions, I weigh the pros and cons and make a rational choice.

Was it hard to choose? On which items? Why? What patterns do we see in our choices? What reasons can you give for your preferences? Did this exercise reveal anything you would like to change about yourself? What?

Pray together the following prayer, followed by the Lord's Prayer: "Holy God, help us as we explore our tendencies to project evil onto others. Help us be honest as we seek to acknowledge our own capacity for evil. We pray as Jesus taught us to pray: 'Our Father. . . .'"

Who Will Be in Charge?

Serena Clark is a young pastor in her first church out of seminary. She soon discovers that one family has dominated the church for years. After her first year, she is ready to suggest some changes in worship, program, and leadership personnel. But whatever she proposes is blocked by Thomas and Corrie Dean and those who support them. Whether it is shifting the offering to after the sermon, organizing a youth retreat, holding a Lenten study, getting a new treasurer, or increasing the mission budget, she always gets responses like "We don't do things like that here," "We can't afford that," "No one will participate," or "The board won't approve it." Serena notes from the church record that for the past thirty years, no pastor has stayed more than three, and now she knows why. She also observes a disturbing pattern of new people visiting a time or two, then not coming back, and she wonders if the underlying tension in the congregation is putting them off. In calling on them, she finds them giving excuses but reluctant to come out and say what bothers them.

Serena wants to be successful in her first church and sees potential for growth and vitality in the young couples coming along. But when she approaches them to take leadership, they beg off with lame excuses. Serena suspects that the Deans' control over every aspect of

> Read "Who Will Be in Charge?" What is the source of conflict in this church? What keeps it from growing? What does Serena want? What do the Deans want? What factors are motivating each? Who is right and who is wrong? Is there evil in the situation? If so, where? What is Satan's goal? Where is God at work? What should happen at the meeting? Role-play the meeting, with persons taking the roles of Serena, the Deans, and the supervisor. Debrief with these questions:
>
> - (To the players) How did you feel in your role? What did you hope to achieve? What would you do differently next time? Where were the crucial turning points? How do you feel about the outcome?
> - (To the group) How did the players do? How would you have handled it differently? What did you hope would happen? What helped or hindered this from taking place? Where did you sense God and Satan at work?

church life is preventing anything creative from happening. Finally, in one board meeting, Serena confronts Thomas Dean, saying, "As pastor of this church, I am called to lead. I hope we can work together toward common goals, but I feel blocked by you at every turn. What do you have against me?" Mr. Dean gets red in the face, mutters, "No pastor can insult me like that and get away with it," gets up, and stomps out. This frightens Serena, and after the meeting, she calls her supervisor and tells him the whole story—only to learn that Dean has already talked with him. The supervisor offers to mediate, and a date is set. Serena prays, "God give me wisdom to know what to say in this meeting."

Our tendency in situations like this is to blame the other for what is going wrong. The Deans blame Serena for trying to upset the applecart, introduce new ideas, disturb their comfort, and wrest control. Serena, full of enthusiasm and new ideas, wants to see things happen, vitality released, and new people become active. She blames the Deans for obstructing progress and quenching the Spirit. Each attributes evil intent to the other and fails to see any fault within themselves.

Assigning Blame in the Bible

While the Hebrews were enslaved in Egypt, longing for their freedom, Moses the liberator arose to confront the tyrant and demand their release. Repeatedly he went before Pharaoh to request their release, but each time he was refused. The explanation given for Pharaoh's obstinacy was that God hardened his heart so he would not let the people go. God subsequently inflicted plagues on the Egyptians. When Pharoah finally did let the people go, the Egyptians chased after them and suffered an awesome defeat at God's hand (Exodus 4:21; 7:3; 14:4, 26-30). The cause of their misery was not a sadistic monarch or a supernatural devil but rather the mysterious will of a sovereign God pursuing a higher purpose. God would be more greatly glorified, the signs and wonders would be more impressive, and the divine judgment would be more decisive if the people just suffered a little longer until the time was ripe. God willed evil so that a greater good might come.

In 1 Samuel 16:14-23, the torment of King Saul is attributed to the departure of God's spirit and the arrival of an evil one. Saul's servants are sent out to look for a skilled musician to soothe his troubled mind with his lyre. "When the evil spirit from God is upon you, he will play it, and you will feel better," Saul is told (16:16). So David is brought in and becomes

Saul's right-hand man. "And whenever the evil spirit from God came upon Saul, David took the lyre and played it with his hand, and Saul would be relieved and feel better, and the evil spirit would depart from him" (16:23).

Note that the spirit, though evil, comes from God. Saul's melancholy or depression is blamed on an evil spirit, but because the almighty God is sovereign over all, it had to come from God. The writer could not countenance anything happening that was outside the will of God. Saul's mental misery was unfortunate, but God must have had a purpose in it. It could be soothed by David's music, but it would not do for it to be cured, for God must have wanted him to endure it. Unlike the cruelty of Pharaoh, which lent itself to God's ultimate victory, the mental anguish of Saul served no higher purpose but was just to be tolerated and temporarily assuaged. Still, though, the authorship of evil lies with God, not Satan.

> Form four teams. Team one should read Exodus 4:21; 7:3; 14:4. Team two should read 1 Samuel 16:14-23. Team three should read Matthew 15:1-20. Team four should read Acts 5:1-11. What is your response to the source of evil as described in the Scriptures? In your experience, who or what is to blame for your sin and suffering—the permission of God, a mysterious evil influence, your own self-centered heart, or the corrupting power of Satan? Which of these are at work in the church of Serena and the Deans?

Matthew 15:1-20 records an encounter between Jesus and the scribes and Pharisees in which Jesus lays full responsibility for evil squarely on the human heart. When they accuse Jesus' disciples of breaking the law, he calls them on their hypocrisy, which honors traditional legalism above its divine intent. Jesus then uses the occasion to demonstrate to the crowd that "it is not what goes into the mouth...but...what comes out...that defiles" (15:11—a reference to dietary laws). When they ask for a further explanation, he gets quite graphic: "Do you not see that whatever goes into the mouth enters the stomach, and goes out into the sewer? But what comes out of the mouth proceeds from the heart, and this is what defiles. For out of the heart come evil intentions, murder, adultery, fornication, theft, false witness, slander. These are what defile a person, but to eat with unwashed hands does not defile" (15:17-20). Thus, according to Jesus, we cannot blame our sinful acts and attitudes on either God or the devil. There is no one to blame but ourselves. Neither Serena Clark nor the Deans can say, "The devil made me do it" or "It's all the other's fault." They must accept full responsibility for both cause and cure of their conflict.

Another instance of assigning blame for evil occurs in the story of Ananias and Sapphira (Acts 5:1-11). In the early days after the Resurrection, the first Christians felt led by God to sell all their possessions, contribute the proceeds to a common treasury, and live together in community. But Ananias and Sapphira withhold part of the sale price of a piece of property and conspire to lie about it. Peter confronts them with the question "Why has Satan filled your heart to lie to the Holy Spirit?" And, their sin thus publicly exposed, both are overcome with guilt and fear, fall down dead, and are carried out to be buried. Here, the source of evil is not God, an evil spirit, or human perfidy; it is Satan, pure and simple. Of course, Ananias and Sapphira have allowed Satan to take control and lead them astray, hence their summary punishment. But it is the power of Satan that seduces them into selfish greed and flagrant deceit, then leaves them to take the rap for it.

Pits, Logs, and Specks

Jesus was addressing these questions when he spoke about judging others while ignoring our own shortcomings. In Luke 6:37-42, he tells us not to condemn others, lest the judgment turn back upon us. If we instead offer forgiveness, we will be forgiven. Hostility begets hostility; love evokes a loving response. If we give generously, we will receive in like measure. When we are blind to our faults and defensively point the finger at another, both of us risk failure (the pit); our relationship and the situation around us are doomed. It is hypocritical to claim we are blameless while accusing the other of spoiling the soup. Evil forces are out to get us; it is we, the pure and innocent, who

Read Luke 6:37-42. In what situations have you tried to claim the white hat role while fixing the black hat on another? What has been the result? What might you do to correct that mistake? In what global situations has this projection of blame been attempted? With what result? How is Satan using this to accomplish his ends? What might God's will be here? What moves might be taken to bring peace and reconciliation? What openings do you see for the Spirit to work?

69

must be protected. If they would just clean up their act, we would be freed up to restore the situation to perfection. It's their fault, not ours. We will even help them become good (remove the speck); but nothing in us needs changing (the log).

When we read these parables and analogies, we tend to use them defensively in ways contrary to what Jesus intended. Phrases such as "Far be it from me to judge, but…" and "He better get his own house in order before talking about mine" do not reflect Jesus' meaning. While people do make judgments, Jesus reminds us that judging people for their faults and frailties is not of God. How can we safely lead someone who cannot see if we are blinded ourselves? How can we help another with a minor fault when we ourselves exhibit a major defect? As followers of Christ, we do not enhance our stature by disparaging the brokenness of others. Putting another down to build ourselves up only reveals our own weakness. Projecting the devilish impulse onto the other while asserting the purity of our own motives is really a device of Satan for hurting persons and perpetuating conflict.

The Struggle Within

In Romans 7:14–8:2, Paul addresses the issue of the source and solution for evil in our hearts and lives from another angle. The depth of his own personal struggle is poignantly expressed in 7:14-24. He is continually battling with an inner tendency to do what he knows is wrong while failing to do the right. He attributes this to being "of the flesh," that is, suffering from human limitations. He has been "sold into slavery" (7:14), a reference to the chattel servitude practiced in Rome under which one human being was owned by another. One was a slave for life unless bought and set free by another. Paul is mystified as to what makes his behavior so inconsistent and undependable, spurning the spiritual law given by God to guide him in the right path (7:15-19). Grasping at straws and apparently not wanting to take the blame on himself, he attributes it to the "sin that dwells within me" (7:20), as though this were something alien to him and for which he is not responsible.

Taylor Caldwell's novel *Great Lion of God* suggests that the youthful Saul of Tarsus had a romantic encounter with a young maiden with whom he fell madly in love—an experience that left him saddled with a burden of guilt for the rest of his life. Of course, this is sheer fiction, and only one fanciful theory about the source of Paul's preoccupation with sin and guilt. Much more likely is the deep remorse he felt for having fiercely persecuted the followers of the Savior who met, forgave, and saved him on the Damascus road.

In his experience as described in Romans, there seems to be a "law" (principle, tendency, disposition) within that prompts him to do the wrong thing. "Evil" (a contrary force: Satan, the devil) is lurking close at hand to lure him off the straight and narrow (7:21). His good self (better judgment) is inspired by God's Word (7:22), but when the rubber hits the road, that other law that "dwells in my members" tends to get the upper hand. Again, he seems to be projecting his sinful tendencies onto a force inhabiting his body that is not the real him but is controlling him (7:23). In other places, however, Paul stresses personal responsibility for sin, which makes this inference questionable (see Romans 1:21-25; 5:12, 14).

> How do you feel about or what do you think about Paul's notion of an evil force within him?

This inner war has made Paul profoundly miserable ("wretched"); he is desperate for deliverance from this "body of death" (a suffocating, destructive, seemingly interminable and inescapable warfare within— 7:24). In his summary assessment of his divided situation, in his mind he is obedient to God's word, but in his flesh he is still controlled by a wayward disposition (7:25b). In other words, it is his intention to do good, but this is continually being undermined by selfish human passions.

But then relief arrives! "Thanks be to God through Jesus Christ our Lord!" (7:25a). The "condemnation"—the heavy sense of judgment and doom—is lifted (8:1). The nagging guilt is swept away. The "law [principle, power, presence of God] of the Spirit of life" liberates us from the "law [influence, allure, force] of

> Divide into teams to study Romans 7:14–8:2. Assign one section to each team: 7:14-20; 7:21-23; 7:24-25; 8:1-2. Read and discuss the assigned Scripture, formulate a one-sentence summary of its central point, and answer this question: How would our lives and society be different if we really took this message seriously? When reporting back, write up the one-sentence summaries in one column and the implications for our lives in another. Invite responses to each other's reports. What steps might we take to put these ideas into practice?

71

sin and death [Satan]" (8:2). It is Christ who makes the difference. Up to the point when he enters the fray, the debilitating struggle has been a standoff. But now, Christ has accomplished what good intentions could not. Christ has smoked out the contrariness lurking within, identified it for the sinister influence it is, and made it possible to resist perverse temptations, fulfill divine expectations, and follow the guidance of the Spirit (8:3-4).

Examining Our Motives

Recall the forced choice exercise with which the session began. Reflection on the Scriptures in this session stimulates questions that can guide us as we examine our motives and ourselves. Is anyone either totally good or totally evil? Is Satan "over there," "in here," or both? What mistakes are caused when we blame the other for our predicaments without recognizing the log in our own eye? Do we allow for a margin of error in our decisions? Do we recognize the inner struggle between the "law of sin" and the "law of God" as we make our choices? Do we sometimes choose to do the very thing we hate? Why? What might we learn by listening to our opponents? Might there be merit in a contrary view that could modify our own for the better? What might we lose by condemning the other without a fair hearing? Are we justified in invariably either condemning or congratulating ourselves? Why might Paul have been so down on himself? What has been the effect on Western civilization—and our mental health—of Christian overemphasis on human depravity following the legacy of Paul? How has Satan made use of this? Might we—as well as the other—be a mixture of the bad and the good? Is consistency a virtue or a vice? How can we know when to trust the advice and example of others and when to keep our own counsel? When is staying our course sheer stubbornness, and when is it a mark of courage?

It is challenging to sort out the causes of happenings in our lives. We are often reluctant to acknowledge mistakes of judgment or willful disobedience on our part. We may feel overwhelmed by forces beyond our control. Some perceive Satan at work, and others attribute events to chance. We know that God is at work in a sinful world, but we do not always know how. We see few signs that we have been "set...free from the law of sin and of death" (Romans 8:2). When we seek God's leading in prayer, we find if difficult to distinguish the guidance of the Spirit from the lure of Satan. We want to be sure that God's wisdom guides us.

Seeking God's wisdom sets us on the right track. Like Paul, we can trust God to be with us and to give us the power to triumph over our own capacity for evil. Through the power of Christ, we can accomplish our good intentions, resist perverse temptations, fulfill divine expectations, and follow the guidance of the Spirit.

Closing Prayer

Following this discussion, join in a prayer circle, arms linked, singing "I Want a Principle Within" and thanking God that for each one in the group, "there is therefore now no condemnation for those who are in Christ Jesus. For the law of the Spirit of life in Christ Jesus has set you free from the law of sin and death" (Romans 8:1-2). Pray together the Lord's Prayer.

CHAPTER 7
CONTENDING AGAINST SATAN

*Where do we find strength to empower
our resistance against Satan?*

Focus: This chapter offers resources to strengthen us in our struggle against evil in our lives and world.

Gathering

Greet one another. Read aloud Ephesians 6:10: "Finally, be strong in the Lord and in the strength of his power." How can a person be strong in the Lord? List some ways. Pray together the Lord's Prayer.

Contending Against Satan in the Kosovo War

Amidst all the barbarism and suffering of the savage Kosovo war some years ago, there were also acts of heroism and compassion. One such act occurred in the town of Decane, where the abbot of the Serbian Orthodox monastery sheltered scores of ethnic Albanian villagers from the brutality of Serb troops. Then, after the soldiers were gone, the monastery became a haven for the Serbian townspeople, protecting them from threats of revenge by the Kosovo Liberation Army.

While the retreating Serb soldiers were robbing, looting, and burning down the mosque, the brave abbot turned the monastery into an oasis of safety and peace for Serbs and Albanians alike. He sent cars to the homes of threatened families to bring 150 Albanians to shelter inside the monastery. In town, monks stood guard outside the gated courtyards of Albanian families who were hidden inside. When the soldiers came looking for them, the monks told them no one was home. What makes this all the more remarkable is that for both Orthodox Christian Serbs and Muslim Albanians, faith and nationality are usually identical. But to Abbot Theodosia, "they were honest people of all faiths and nations," and to save them from violence was "the Christian thing to do, the human thing to do. We are happy we could help them."

Throughout the fighting, the abbot aided the Albanians, giving them food, visiting their homes, and asking them on the street if they were all right. "They risked their lives for us," said one Albanian of the monks. Remembering the monastery's courage and kindness in harboring them, the local Albanians, who were Muslim, vowed to protect the monks. One villager said, "If they are going to kill them, they must kill us first. They saved us." One day, Serb soldiers came to the monastery gate, but not to force their way in. Instead, they told the monks barring their way that they had come to pray for forgiveness for what they had done.[1]

> Read Ephesians 6:10-20. Compare the story of Abbot Theodosia and his monks with the elements in the armor of God described there. In what ways were the monks "strong in the Lord and in the strength of his power" (6:10)? How did they "stand against the wiles of the devil, … the cosmic powers of this present darkness" (6:11-12)? How did "the whole armor of God" help them "stand firm" (6:13) in protecting the innocent? In what ways did the armor of truth, righteousness, peace, faith, and salvation; the sword of the Spirit; and the power of prayer empower them "to make known with boldness the mystery of the gospel" (6:19)?

The Whole Armor of God

The Letter to the Ephesians concludes with advice about the tools believers need in the struggle against evil. Christians must be equipped with the power of God (6:10-17) and pray for each other in their conflict with the powers so they can witness boldly (6:18-20). In verse 10, the Greek word translated *finally* literally means "henceforth" or "in the future." If they are to cope successfully with coming trials, they must be properly equipped. "Be strong" is to be taken in the passive sense of "be made powerful." That is, we cannot handle it on our own; we should let

God empower us. In verse 11, God offers Christians equipment ("armor of God") to enable us to stand up against the powers of evil. The "wiles of the devil" refer to the many temptations to sin, unfaithfulness, and accommodation to pagan society with which Christians have been confronted, then and now.

The first-century worldview peopled the universe with a fearsome host of angels, demons, and evil spirits, which in verse 12 are spoken of as rulers, authorities, cosmic powers, and the "spiritual forces of evil in the heavenly places." The enemies of these early Christians were not only "blood and flesh" human beings but also profoundly evil spiritual beings of overwhelming might.

While this understanding was likely influenced by the pantheon of Greek and Roman gods and goddesses feared and worshiped by the ancients, it points to a reality as true today as long ago. Political, economic, and cultural structures partake of a spiritual ethos greater than the sum of their parts. An institution has a corporate personality that affects for good or ill all who relate to it. Every government, corporation, university, or sports team (principality or power) is characterized by a particular spirit or climate that can be located along a continuum between life-giving and life-suffocating. We may not think of these powers as personal beings as they did in the first century, but they are real nevertheless—and larger than life.

Walter Wink describes these "demons" as the actual spirituality of systems and structures that have betrayed their divine vocations—" 'the Domination System' [as]…an entire network of Powers…integrated around idolatrous values,…[and] 'Satan' as the world-encompassing spirit of the Domination System."[2] The thesis of his trilogy on the Powers is that they are first good, then fallen, and finally must be redeemed.

We can imagine how powerless the early Christians must have felt as they—a tiny minority in a hostile pagan world—took on the challenge of proclaiming the gospel and living an alternative lifestyle surrounded by the active opposition of both their human neighbors and rulers and these superhuman powers. To triumph against these odds was impossible in their own strength; they needed "the whole armor of God." The Roman soldier—agent of an evil, oppressive empire—was a common sight in every city and highway, his uniform and weapons familiar to everyone. So Ephesians 6:11 draws on this analogy of the implements of resistance and protection to detail the equipment that God provides the believer in the struggle against the powers. The use of weapon metaphors to speak of

God's battle against evil is also found in the Old Testament. (See Isaiah 11:5 and 59:16-17). In the latter passage, Yahweh himself is arrayed in some of the same pieces of armor mentioned here.

The "evil day" (Ephesians 6:13) may refer to the common first-century belief that the time was fast approaching when the powers of evil would be lined up against the forces of good in a final, cataclysmic battle that would bring the destruction of the world and the triumph of righteousness. (See 2 Thessalonians 2:8-10; Revelation 16:12-16; 20:7-8.) But the evil day can also be personalized to mean the times of testing that everyone seeking to be faithful to Christ in a sinful world must face.[3]

The first resource for this struggle is the "belt of truth" (Ephesians 6:14a). The soldier's belt fastens his tunic and holds up his sword, thus freeing him to move swiftly and decisively. The believer, remembering that Jesus said, "I am the way, and the truth, and the life" (John 14:6) and "You will know the truth, and the truth will make you free" (John 8:32), will find the security and freedom to speak courageously and act resolutely through a firm commitment to Jesus Christ.

The "breastplate" (Ephesians 6:14b)—or, as one translator puts it, the "bulletproof vest"[4]—protects the heart and other vital organs from the thrusts of the enemy. For the Christian, this protection comes from "righteousness"—a life of integrity. Attacks against one who lives above reproach have little effect, for the witness of honor and good character is hard to undermine. This requires faithfully resisting temptation and choosing the right path, which is impossible to do consistently in one's own strength alone. So God through Christ empowers us to be steadfast in the struggle.

The "shoes" (6:15) in this uniform of the faithful Christian are the equipment for sharing the good news of "peace." It is ironic that peace is the message that the warrior for Christ is called to proclaim. But just as Jesus was condemned to a violent death for advocating the ways of peace, so ever since have those who practice loving, nonviolent resistance to evil aroused the wrath of the forces of violence. Shoes enable one to move quickly through rough territory, travel long distances without soreness, and stand for peace, speak for Christ, and act for justice in his name.

The "shield" (6:16) that protects us from the darts of temptation and the spears of accusation is "faith"—a relationship of trust in the God who loves and cares for us. Many Christians lost their lives in the early persecutions, so this does not mean that faith in God enables us to escape trials and suffering. It goes deeper than that. It is the kind of faith that affirms with Paul, "We know that all things work together for good for those who love God, who are called according to his purpose.... If God is for us, who is against us?...Who will separate us from the love of Christ? Will hardship, or distress, or persecution, or famine, or nakedness, or peril, or sword?... No, in all these things we are more than conquerors through him who loved us. For I am convinced that neither death, nor life, nor angels, nor rulers, nor things present, nor things to come, nor powers, nor height, nor depth, nor anything else in all creation, will be able to separate us from the love of God in Christ Jesus our Lord" (Romans 8:28, 31, 35, 37-39). The shield of this kind of faith may not stop a bullet, ward off racist taunts, or prevent a prison sentence for civil disobedience against an unjust law. But it will empower us to overcome the fear of rejection, hurt, or death in order to remain true to God's justice and concern for the well-being of all.

Next is the "helmet of salvation" (Ephesians 6:17a). The verb *take* here literally means "accept," suggesting that the helmet and sword are gifts of God, not acquisitions of the human will. When Paul quoted Isaiah 59:17 in 1 Thessalonians 5:8, he changed this phrase to the helmet of "the hope of salvation." For him, salvation was not something already achieved. Rather, it was the anticipated culmination of a process begun in Christ's sacrifice on the cross and continued by the Spirit's activity in the life of individual believers and in the course of history leading toward an ultimate consummation. It is this hope that sustains us in the ongoing struggle against evil. For we know that even if our individual efforts are unsuccessful, the final triumph of God's righteousness is assured.

The "sword of the Spirit" (Ephesians 6:17b) provided to the Christian battling against the powers is the "word of God." This phrase has a double meaning, referring both to the Bible and to Jesus Christ, "the Word [that] became flesh" (John 1:14). Certainly the revelation of God in Scripture is a means for nurturing our spirits and strengthening our wills to persevere in the struggle. But Scripture is given to point us to Christ, the supreme revelation of God's love and purpose for humankind. So the ultimate resource in the contest with evil is the love embodied in Jesus Christ, who empowers us and gives himself for us so that we, like him, may be faithful to the end.

The last tool mentioned is prayer (Ephesians 6:18-20). The kind of prayer that will be effective in the struggle against the powers has five qualities. First, it must be "in the Spirit"—in other words, in the Spirit of Jesus, the spirit of love and goodwill. Prayers condemning others or implying one's spiritual superiority at the expense of others are not worthy of a follower of Christ. We must invoke the forgiving, compassionate, reconciling Spirit of Jesus in our praying. Second, our prayer should be fervent and passionate ("keep alert"). Lackadaisical petitions with little expectation of an answer will get us nowhere. Third, it must be continuous ("always persevere"). Sporadic prayer will not do; we must keep at it. Fourth, our prayer must express concern and support for all of God's people ("the saints.") Intercessory prayer—asking God to care for and strengthen the witness of sisters and brothers both here and abroad—is basic to the solidarity of the universal body of Christ. And finally, the goal of such prayer is empowerment for bold proclamation of the good news in word and deed.

> Read Ephesians 6:13-20. Explore the meaning of each element in "the whole armor of God." How do we acquire them? Are they gifts of God or virtues acquired through effort? Is the use of such military metaphors inconsistent with the spiritual qualities the writer is trying to emphasize? Why or why not? Which of them come naturally, and which are hard to embody?

In the struggle between Satan and the Spirit, then, taking on "the whole armor of God" empowers us to contend against evil and witness for good. Empowerment or being strong means more than mustering our courage. It suggests receiving a power beyond our own. We can accept the "breastplate of righteousness" in order not only to *do* right but also to *make* things right. Our "shield of faith" is our trusting relationship with God.

Other Biblical Resources

In addition to the Ephesians passage, the New Testament points to other resources for contending against Satan. Luke 9 begins with Jesus giving the disciples authority over demons and diseases, then sending them forth to herald the reign of God and restore to wholeness those who have been broken by Satan's power. When the seventy return from a similar mission, they gladly report, "Lord, in your name even the demons submit to us!" to which Jesus replies that he has seen Satan fall from heaven and has given them authority to stomp on "snakes and scorpions"—symbols of the "power of the enemy"—so they will be safe from harm (Luke 10:17-20). Claiming the authority of Jesus by speaking and acting in his name

Read Luke 9, Ephesians 4:26-27, James 2:18-26, James 4:7-8, and 1 Peter 5:6-11. Identify the resources for our struggle against Satan offered in each. Compare these with the resources many people turn to in search of help and guidance: psychotherapy, support and self-help groups, drugs and tranquilizers, twelve-step programs, television and movies, popular gurus, sects and cults, and so forth. What is the appeal of these sources of strength and help? Are they effective? Why or why not? How can we get a handle on the "whole armor of God" and the other resources discussed in this chapter as sources of power for the struggle against evil?

empowers us in the struggle against the demonic. The witness against evil may lead us into places of physical danger, but our spiritual integrity and soul's salvation will be preserved.

Ephesians 4:26-27 advises, "Be angry but do not sin; do not let the sun go down on your anger, and do not make room for the devil." Prophetic indignation against the forces and effects of evil, grounded in an inner sense of justice and commitment to protect God's children, is an authentic source of power—so long as we do not harbor grudges, malign our opponents personally, or use the devil's own methods in opposing his legions.

In James 2:18-26, the importance of combining faith with good works is stressed. Belief alone is insufficient; even the demons know the truth about God but tremble in fear before the divine presence, knowing their actions negate this truth. Deeds of kindness, justice, humility, and love (see Micah 6:8) directly counter the aims of Satan, undermine his rule, and point to the reign of God, which is already among us (see Luke 17:21). James further counsels, "Submit yourselves therefore to God. Resist the devil, and he will flee from you. Draw near to God, and he will draw near to you. Cleanse your hands, you sinners, and purify your hearts, you double-minded" (James 4:7-8). If we trust God and follow God's ways, God will sustain us in the struggle. If we openly defy Satan, he will slink away. If we practice the presence of God, the Spirit will envelope us. If we acknowledge our ambivalence and lack of fortitude, forgiveness, affirmation, and guidance will be supplied.

In 1 Peter 5:6-11, we are told that when we humble ourselves before God, trust God with our worries, discipline ourselves, stay alert, stand in solidarity with our comrades in the struggle, and refuse to give up, we will be sustained. Thus, although "like a roaring lion your adversary the devil prowls around, looking for someone to devour," we will be empowered to resist him and need not fear. The God we serve will "restore, support, strengthen, and establish" us, for in him is "the power forever and ever. Amen."

In this study, we have confronted several issues associated with the figure of the devil and the problem of evil, and we have explored ways God offers strength and power to deal with each of the issues. In Chapter 1, "The Problem of Evil," we asked where evil comes from and examined the manifestations and sources of evil in our lives and world, as well as the roles assigned to Satan as the cause of evil. In Chapter 2, "Satan as Tempter," we explored the experience of temptation and the faith resources for dealing with it. Chapter 3, "Satan as Fallen Angel and Adversary," explored the relationship between God and Satan

> What have you learned? How have your faith and commitment been strengthened? What questions remain? What are the next steps that God is calling you to make in your life of discipleship?

(good and evil), in biblical accounts, Christian and ancient Near Eastern traditions, and human experience in seeking answers to the question if Satan is independent of or subordinate to God. "Demon Possession and Exorcism" was the focus of Chapter 4, which, in response to the question of who can calm the troubled spirit, related the experience of demon possession and exorcism in biblical times and traditional societies to contemporary forms of mental illness and healing. Turning to "The Antichrist and the End Times," Chapter 5 addressed the question of what the future holds and who holds the future by exploring biblical perspectives on the antichrist in relation to Satan, end-times beliefs, the second coming of Christ, the teachings of Jesus, and Christian hope. Chapter 6, "The Devil in 'the Other'—And in Us," raised the question of who is to blame and confronted the human tendency to project evil onto "the other," as well as the need to acknowledge its presence within us. Now, in this final chapter, "Contending Against Satan," we have addressed the question of where we find the strength to empower our resistance against Satan. We have examined resources to empower us in our struggle against evil in all its forms.

"Get Behind Me, Satan!"

Thus, as we contend against evil, we are empowered by God to use the words of Jesus, "Get behind me, Satan!" Jesus knew that in his struggle against the powers in Jerusalem, he had to face suffering and death. When Peter remonstrated that things could not possibly be that bad, Jesus sensed the devil tempting him to seek an easier way out, using Peter's friendly concern to divert him from his central mission. So he used strong words to rebuke his disciple: "Get behind me, Satan"—stumbling block, tempter, adversary, Lucifer, Beelzebul, Belial, enemy of God (see Matthew 16:21-23).

The human mind seeks security and self-preservation; the mind of God calls for devotion to salvation, liberation, and justice for all. For Jesus, this required redemptive suffering and death, but through Jesus, God offers redemption, new life, and the reign of God. As we seek God's way of being in the world, we are empowered to resist and overcome evil.

Closing Worship

Sing "Lead On, O King Eternal" or "Stand By Me." Then repeat the baptismal vows cited in the introduction of this book:

- Do you renounce the spiritual forces of wickedness, reject the evil powers of this world, and repent of your sin? *Response:* **I do.**

- Do you accept the freedom and power God gives you to resist evil, injustice, and oppression in whatever forms they present themselves? *Response:* **I do.**

- Do you confess Jesus Christ as your Savior, put your whole trust in his grace, and promise to serve him as your Lord, in union with the church which Christ has opened to people of all ages, nations, and races? *Response:* **I do.**[5]

Close by praying in unison: "O God, help us to say 'Get behind me, Satan' in every aspect of our lives. Help us to contend against Satan with every fiber of our being. In our struggle against evil, give us your resources of (name gifts and practices mentioned in this session). Through Jesus Christ our Lord. Amen."

Notes

[1] See the following websites: http://www.incommunion.org/articles/news-reports/monastic-peacemaking-in-kosovo; http://www.incommunion.org/articles/resources/for-the-peace-from-above/chapter-8; http://www.kosovo.com/decani_peace.html.

[2] From *Engaging the Powers,* by Walter Wink (Fortress Press, 1992); pages 8–9.

[3] See *The New Interpreter's Bible,* Vol. XI (Abingdon Press, 2000); pages 460–61.

[4] From *The Cotton Patch Version of Paul's Epistles,* by Clarence Jordan (Association Press, 1968); page 114.

[5] From *The United Methodist Hymnal* (The United Methodist Publishing House, 1989); page 34.